Serial Chase

A true story of the lives and deaths
of a doctor and a deputy

Neil Bradley Hampson, MD

Cover photo licensed from Colourbox.com #46292 4/5/2013.

Neil B. Hampson MD

PREFACE

Neil B. Hampson: "Ever since I can remember, my grandmother, Helen R. Hart, was married to her second husband, William W. Hart. As a child, my mother told me that her natural father—Helen's first husband—had died when she was in college at the University of Washington. At an early age, I was told that the cause of his death was a heart attack. When I was in high school, she told me "the truth." As I recall, she said that he was an alcoholic and was out drinking in an Everett, Washington, bar. He liked to show off his prosperity and laid a large roll of bills on the counter while sitting there. Someone apparently saw the money, and when he left the bar, the person shot and robbed him. The murderer was never caught."

Diane K. Hampson (Neil's wife): "I was told that Russell Bradley was an alcoholic, was out drinking one night, and was found dead by strangulation on the side of a road. The murderer was caught and sent to prison. There was no mention of money or a gun."

Carole J. Hampson (Neil's sister): "I remember Mom telling me that he was at the Elks Club in Everett gambling, and he met a man and they left together. (I don't remember if she said he drove him home or not.) I think she said our grandfather was found on a country road, strangled and dead. She seemed to imply they thought it was because our grandfather had won big money gambling and someone robbed him. For years she said he died of a heart attack."

David F. Hampson (Neil's brother): "What I remember is that he was at a bar on one of his several-day binges, got a ride home with a cab driver, and was robbed and strangled to death. Everyone thought he died of a heart attack. Then a year later, when the cab driver was convicted of another murder, he admitted to two others, one being Russell's. They then dug him up, reexamined him, and confirmed that he had been strangled."

CHAPTER 1

It was growing late in the evening on a cold, misty Monday night in December 1950. However, things were bright and lively inside the lobby of the plush Monte Cristo Hotel at 1507 Wall Street in Everett, Washington. The elegant Monte Cristo, located in the center of downtown, had a lobby bar frequented by the city's more prosperous citizens. A handful of well-dressed couples were having cocktails at tables around the edge of the round white marble-floor, chatting loudly about the details of the piano concert they had just attended.

The bar itself was a room that arose off the right side of the lobby. Lighting there was more subdued, the bar and tables stained a dark maple color, and a thick carpet covered the floor, soaking up spilled drinks and the details of private conversations. Two men sat beside one another at the bar, chatting, laughing at the jokes of the other, and sipping their drinks. They could not have looked less likely to be together. One was a 52-year-old successful local businessman, 5 feet 10 inches tall, and slight in build. He was a well-known and liked optometrist who lived in Everett but maintained offices in other towns of the region, as well. He wore a dark blue pinstripe suit with a Masonic Temple pin on the lapel and did not wear eyeglasses. He smoked cigarettes one after another. During the evening, a group of Shriners leaving the bar stopped to talk with the man, clapped him on the back and shook his hand, thanking him for the holiday season dinner party that he had hosted for the fraternal group at his waterfront weekend home the preceding Saturday.

On the bar stool next to him is a clean-cut young man who was recently discharged from the US Army. At six-foot-one and 230 pounds, he dwarfs the older man. He was wearing the uniform of the Snohomish County Sheriff's posse, into which he was deputized a year earlier even though he fell short of the minimum age requirement. He wore wire rim eyeglasses.

The men are talking and laughing, and the optometrist is happy to buy a few rounds for the young sheriff's deputy. In fact, he pulls out a large roll of bills and privately shows only the deputy to demonstrate that he's well able to afford it. When the conversation turns to women, the older man suggests that they drive to a brothel in Marysville, where they can continue to party. He cashes a $20 check to pay the bar tab. But when he stands up, he staggers.

The deputy immediately offers to drive him home. He asks the bartender to help him get the optometrist into his Chevy pickup, which is parked out front. The bartender goes back into the hotel as the men drive off.

An hour later, the Chevy pulls up in front of Everett General Hospital's emergency entrance. The driver is distraught; his passenger is dead.

Hospital personnel accept the explanation that the optometrist suffered a heart attack en route. Thirteen months later, his body is exhumed and autopsied, and the conclusion is much different.

The optometrist was my grandfather, and the truth about his death is chilling. The truth is that a serial killer and arsonist fooled psychiatrists, physicians, and military and law enforcement officials long enough to commit crimes in at least three states, for which he served less than a decade in prison.

CHAPTER 2

E arly on the morning of Tuesday, December 12, 1950, repeated knocking on the front door awakened my grandmother, Helen R. Bradley. She got up, put on her robe, and turned on the lights. Standing on the porch were Sheriff's Deputy Clarence DeMars, County Coroner Ken Baker, and another man, Mr. Harold Chase, Special Deputy with the Snohomish County Sheriff's Posse. They relayed the information that her husband, Dr. Russell R. Bradley, had died that evening. It was explained that Chase and Bradley had met one another at the bar in the Monte Cristo Hotel in downtown Everett, about two blocks from Bradley's optometry office. After several drinks over the course of the evening, Bradley became intoxicated and was deemed by the bartender to be too impaired to drive safely.

Chase, twenty-one, volunteered to drive him home, and the bartender helped Chase load Dr. Bradley into the passenger seat of Chase's pickup. On the way to Dr. Bradley's home, he appeared to have a heart attack, according to Chase. He drove immediately to Everett General Hospital's emergency entrance. However, Bradley was found to be dead upon arrival. Chase expressed sympathy and his sorrow that he was unable to help him.

The single-page Snohomish County coroner's record for case no. 50-208-809, Russell R. Bradley, states his cause of death to be coronary thrombosis secondary to coronary sclerosis. No autopsy was performed. The form lists his place of death to be in an auto at 1321 Colby Avenue, the address of the hospital where he was pronounced dead in the truck. No names are listed under "witnesses," despite the fact that he was in a vehicle owned and driven to the hospital by Mr. Harold Chase. At one place on the form, it lists the address for Dr. and Mrs. Bradley correctly. At another, it lists Mrs. Bradley living at the address for the hospital. Under "Results of Investigation," only two words are written in a portion of the page ruled for twenty lines of text: "natural death."

Russell R. Bradley's death certificate, signed by his personal physician, Dr. R. B. Townsend, lists the official cause of death as "coronary thrombosis due to coronary sclerosis." In lay terms, he had a heart attack.

Daughter Mary Louise came home from the University of Washington, where she was a student, and son Richard was given leave from his job with the Navy Transport Service. A funeral service was held for Dr. Bradley three days later at Trinity Episcopal Church in Everett. An escort of Knights Templar attended. His body was entombed at View Crest Abbey mausoleum, named presumably because of the facility's hilltop location and its view overlooking Smith Island to the north of Everett.

Eventually, life moved on. Helen was remarried to William W. Hart, with whom she would eventually celebrate her second silver wedding anniversary. Richard returned to school and became an optometrist like his father. Mary Louise graduated from the University of Washington, got married, and became my mother in 1955.

Russell R. Bradley had been born in Kalispell, Montana, only fifty-two years before meeting Mr. Harold Chase in the Monte Cristo Hotel bar that 1950 December night.

CHAPTER 3

My great-grandfather, Richard N. Bradley, was born in Oregon in 1867 to settlers who came west on the Oregon Trail in a covered wagon from North Carolina and Virginia. His future wife, Edith Manary, was born in 1876 in Ontario, Canada, of parents born in the same city. Richard and Edith were married in Oregon City, Oregon, on October 3, 1895. Their first child, a daughter named Vernettia, was born in Oregon City exactly a year later.

Within two years after Vernettia's birth, the family had moved to Kalispell, Montana, at the north end of Flathead Lake. Richard Bradley apparently moved his wife and baby daughter there because of the promise of work in the area. He began working for the US Forest Service. Richard loved to hunt, and he loved the outdoors. When Glacier became a national park in 1910, he was one of the original rangers. Later in life, it is said that he collected the Great Northern Railroad calendar portraits of those Native Americans he had known while working at Glacier as a ranger.

My grandfather, Russell R. Bradley, was born in Kalispell in 1898. The family was very poor. His mother, Edith, was said to be able to make gravy out of virtually anything, serving over bread for dinner many nights. Russell would hop the trains coming through town and sell newspapers to passengers. His father taught him to hunt. He was very athletic. He was on the high school track team and, as a senior, was one of five Montana high school players named to the all-state basketball team.

While Russell was in high school in Kalispell, he met a Miss Helen Russell Thompson, who was visiting from Wisconsin. Helen was born in 1900 in Red Rock, Wisconsin. When she was two, her family moved to Moscow, Idaho, as her father searched for better farming opportunities. Helen started school in Moscow. The family subsequently moved to Montana as homesteaders about 1910, and then to Turtle Lake, Wisconsin, in 1914. Because there was no high school in diminutive Turtle Lake, Helen attended boarding school in Saint Paul, Minnesota, seventy-one miles away, an experience she bitterly despised. When her best friend, Molly Klaskey, moved to Kalispell, Helen took the train west one summer to visit her. While in Kalispell, she was introduced to Russell Bradley, a young man two years her elder. Their meeting must have gone spectacularly well because it initiated a long-term correspondence after Helen returned home to start college at the University of Minnesota.

Russell R. Bradley as a high school senior, one of five
players named to the Montana all-state basketball team.

CHAPTER 4

Two years after Russell finished high school in 1916, the entire family, including a brother, Walter, who was four years younger than Russell, moved to Seattle for the economic opportunities it offered. They lived at 907 James Street, approximately the site of the current Harborview Medical Center. The children, ages eighteen to twenty-four, were all single and living with their parents. Richard Bradley worked as a timber broker, probably a logical job for a former national park ranger. His daughter, Vernettia, worked as a bookkeeper.

In January 1919, Russell (twenty-two) and Walter (eighteen) went to work in the merchant marine and successfully sailed the world, eventually leaving that service in August 1920. What follows are selected entries from one of Russell's personal handwritten journals:

S. S. Egremont sailed from Seattle December 13, 1919 with flour for New York. Arrived Balboa, Panama January 4, 1920. Left for New York January 7, arriving the 13th.

February 20. Arrived Newport News, Virginia. Loaded 10,000 tons of coal and sailed for Cristobal, Colon (Panama) February 24.

April 7. No such day as today. We went over the 180 degree meridian last night so we jumped one day ahead.

April 23. In South China Sea and west coast of Luzon Island.

April 24. Reached Manila 12 a.m.

May 9. Sailed from Manila for Calcutta 2960 miles.

May 10. On Saturday, May 4, 1920, steward on S.S. Egremont got $29.37 ½ for the following articles which he never delivered: 10 under-shirts @ $0.50 ($5.00) and 25 cartons of cigarettes @ $0.97 ½ ($24.37 ½).

May 17. 3 degrees from equator.

May 18. Some heat. 122 degrees outdoors.

May 19. Fine day. 119 degrees outdoors.

May 22. Going up Ganges River.

May 23. Arrived in Calcutta, India.

June 24. Crossed the equator last night and going north.

June 26. Fine weather. Near Africa. Islands in sight Eastern coast of Africa.

July 3. Red Sea. Egypt one side and Holy Land on other.

July 4. An excitable 4th. 120 degrees and not a breeze blowing.

July 29. Passed Gibraltor (sic) midnight.

July 30. Expect to make the States in 2 weeks.

August 8. High sea. 5 boys are sick. Ship listed 31 degrees. Strong westerly winds. Making 4 miles an hour.

August 12. Arrived Newport News (Virginia). Laying in harbor at anchor. No shore liberty.

August 16. Payed (sic) for 6 months and 6 days from New York. Everyone happy.

Total wages January 1, 1919 to January 1, 1920:

January 1–March 18	Sailor $75 per month	$195
April 3–June 3	Sailor $75 per month	$150
August 5–September 20	(illegible) helper	$132
December 20–January 1, 1920	$2.17 a day O.S.	$62.90
Total wages 1 year		$499.90

Russell Bradley in 1919
(age twenty-one) as a merchant seaman.

CHAPTER 5

Throughout his world travels, Russell Bradley and Helen Thompson continued their correspondence. A letter written by Russell's mother to Helen at the University of Minnesota illustrates how difficult communication was at the time:

Seattle, Wash.
May 10, 1919

Dear Miss Thompson,

We received word Thursday through the U.S. Shipping Board here, that S.S. Brookenhoff (the ship Russell is on) was passing through the Panama Canal that day and all ok. Walter says it will take them ten or twelve more days to get to New York. Then they will have to go up the Hudson River to Poughkeepsie, NY. Walter also says if you will write to Russell at Poughkeepsie, NY c/o U.S. Shipping Board and aboard S.S. Brookenhoff and also write to New York c/o U.S. Shipping Board and aboard S.S. Brookenhoff, he is sure to get one or the other or probably both.

I would also think it advisable for you to leave your present address at the place where you did reside and tell them should Russell come there to direct him.

Russell told me before he left here that he intended to go to St. Paul on his way back to see you.

I hope that you have success in reaching him and that he has a safe trip and no trouble finding you.

Yours lovingly,
Mrs. R.N. Bradley
Box 647
Seattle, Wash.

Russell's communications to Helen over a year and a half demonstrate the progression of their relationship.

Western Union Telegram February 18, 1920

Dearest Helen, Leaving for Norfolk tomorrow. Got out of dry dock. Today received both letters. Am well as usual. Write me at Norfolk and at Colon, Panama. Will write later. With love, Russell Bradley.

Western Union Telegram August 17, 1920

Dearest Helen, Arrived in Norfolk Saturday. Had a fine but rough trip on Atlantic. Leaving there tomorrow for New York. For St. Paul after. Will get there about Saturday. Hope you are well. Russell Bradley

Letter from Russell to Helen September 2, 1920

God's Country

Dearest Helen,

I have been home five days now. I haven't heard a word from you yet. I hope you are not sick but if you are not, then what is your idea for not writing? It is eight days since I left St. Paul. I'm not mad Helen, or got any foolish ideas in my head about you not writing but I am awful anxious to hear from you.

Dad bought a place on Lake Washington while I was away. I have been helping him the last four days getting it in shape for next spring. I have 2 prospects for a job with Wells Fargo Express Co. here at $155 a month. I hope I can land it but not sure for a few days yet. I'll get some kind of a job yet and make our fortune soon as I decide what to do.

Well, Miss Helen Thompson at 1235 Lincoln Avenue, I'll close this short letter to mail it this afternoon. Write often as you can Sweetheart. Lots and lots of love,

Russell xxx

Letter from Russell to Helen October 16, 1921

Dearest Helen:

I want and love you Sweetheart more than anyone in the whole world. This is a very simple little letter just so you will know I am thinking of you this Sunday evening.

Would love to see my dear little girl tonight and love her so much. I have only one sheet of paper but will give you a very bit of love and lots and lots of kisses.

Always yours,
Russell xxxxxxxxxxxxxxxxxxxxxxxxxxxxxx

Helen completed one year at the University of Minnesota, then remained in Saint Paul to work. She must have gone to school on a scholarship that year because her family certainly could not afford to pay college tuition, and none of her four siblings attended college. In the summer of 1922, Helen took a trip to Seattle and did not return home to the Midwest. This was because she married Russell Bradley in Seattle on September 22, 1922. Although they would not make their fortune from it, Russell did find a job. He became a Seattle streetcar conductor, working the Queen Anne counterbalance route.

Queen Anne Avenue goes up Queen Anne Hill out of downtown Seattle. It is an eight-block section of roadway with an average grade of approximately 10 percent from the bottom to the top. However, there is one block with a grade that approaches 20 percent. Prior to 1900, Seattle had cable cars similar to those still seen in San Francisco today. They were capable of climbing such steep grades. In 1901, Seattle switched to electric streetcars. When electric service was proposed to replace the cable cars on Queen Anne Avenue, engineers were faced with the problem that electric streetcars of the early 1900s could only negotiate an uphill grade of approximately 5 percent.

Since no one who lived on top of Queen Anne Hill was interested in walking up the steep slope for the rest of his life, something had to be done. The solution was the "counterbalance." The counterbalance was sixteen tons of concrete on railway wheels, permanently attached to one end of a long steel cable. The counterbalance ran on an underground track beneath Queen Anne Avenue. When an electric streetcar approached the bottom of Queen Anne Hill from downtown, it would stop and connect to the other end of the cable, which was passed around a pulley. The counterbalance, on top of the hill at this point, would be released. It would roll downhill, helping to pull the streetcar uphill. When the streetcar reached the top of the hill and the counterbalance the bottom, the cable was disconnected and the streetcar would continue under electric power atop Queen Anne Hill. When a streetcar going in the opposite direction faced descending the steep hill that was Queen Anne Avenue, it connected to the counterbalance and could make the descent under control, pulling the underground counterbalance back up the hill.

While this solved the immediate problem, the counterbalance was not perfect. Since using the counterbalance required that it be at the opposite end of the grade, two streetcars going in the same direction could not negotiate the hill consecutively. Even worse, when the crew forgot to connect the cable to a streetcar going downhill or the cable broke, the ride was said to be especially harrowing. It is not recorded in family lore whether Russell was ever involved with one of those rapid descents when he worked the counterbalance route.

As an historical aside, this is the reason that some old-timers in Seattle still refer to the south end of Queen Anne Hill as the counterbalance. The tracks upon which the streetcars rode were removed from the streets decades ago when buses took over downtown transportation. The actual counterbalance itself, however, still sits on its tracks in a tunnel beneath Queen Anne Avenue. When it snows in Seattle, the street must be closed because automobiles cannot negotiate the grade—not because of lack of power like the electric streetcars, but because of insufficient traction.

Russell Bradley (on left) in Seattle streetcar conductor's uniform, circa 1922, when he worked the counterbalance route.

CHAPTER 6

Seeing that they would not prosper on a streetcar conductor's salary, even one that was earned on the exciting counterbalance route, Russell set out to get more education by taking night classes at the Seattle YMCA. He also helped support them by working as a hat model. While it seems amazing today, Russell learned the profession of optometry through these night classes and assumed the attendant title of doctor. He opened his first optical office in the small town of Stanwood, about sixty miles north of Seattle. Russell and Helen lived in the community, comprised largely of Scandinavian immigrants who were attracted by the fishing, logging, and farmlands that were similar to those of their home countries.

Russell was very industrious and his practice grew rapidly. When it began to peak in size, he opened a second office in the larger town of Arlington, about twenty miles to the east, toward the Cascade Mountain Range. He split his time between the two offices, thereby providing optical services to the population of a large geographic area. A 1926 survey of businesspeople in Arlington indicated there was one optician working in town, presumably R. R. Bradley. By 1930, he had opened yet another office in the community of Snohomish, located about halfway between Arlington and the city of Everett. Because of his gregarious nature and magnetic personality, his patients loved him, and they were very loyal to him. He was able to close the Stanwood office, as his patients were willing to travel a moderate distance to continue seeing him.

At the time of the 1930 US Census, Russell (thirty-two) and Helen (thirty) were living in Snohomish with their two-year-old son, Russell Richard Bradley Jr. Later that year, their daughter, Mary Louise, was born. According to Russell's son, my uncle, Russell Sr. continued his entrepreneurialism by starting a tamale factory in Snohomish with his friend, Gib Turner. However, in discussing this with present-day representatives of the Snohomish Historical Society, it seems more likely that the two may have produced tamales and had them canned by Ferguson Foods, the major canned-goods producer in the area.

Russell's optometry practice continued to thrive, and in 1935, he opened a new office in Everett, Washington, closing the most distant practice in Arlington. Everett was a thriving port and mill town with the largest population base of any community north of Seattle to the Canadian border. He continued to work in Everett until his death fifteen years later in 1950.

CHAPTER 7

Russell Bradley became an extremely successful businessman and a popular community figure in Everett. His optometry practice drew patients not only from the metropolitan area, but also from the surrounding region, where he had previously established practices. In fact, his practice was the largest in the State of Washington, according to the vendors of eyeglass components. All of them said that his practice consumed more of their products than that of any other optometrist they called upon.

Russell was also active in the community's fraternal circles. He was a member of Alpha Lodge No. 212, Free and Accepted Masons; Palestine Commandery No. 11, Knights Templar; Columbia Chapter No. 33, Order of the Eastern Star; Trinity Episcopal Church; the Rotary Club; Nile Temple Shrine; and the Everett Elks.

In addition to his involvement with the business organizations and fraternal societies of Everett, Russell was a community supporter. During World War II, a nationwide rubber drive was conducted to help ease the rubber shortage caused by the war. In Everett, donated rubber helped to support the local USO by providing cigarettes and candy for servicemen who frequented the clubrooms. Russell had scattered old tires all over a farm that he owned at the time. He was saving them for use in burning out tree stumps. Instead, with the aid of his son, Dick, he borrowed a truck from the Firestone Company, and the two made a field day of searching for rubber. They scoured the entire property for tires and other forms of rubber, often wading deep into murky pools of water to rescue partially submerged tire carcasses. At the end of the day, they presented local drive organizers with 4,000 pounds of old tires and other rubber-containing articles—by far the biggest donation from any individual in the community.

Russell R. Bradley, successful businessman and popular
community figure in Everett, Washington.

CHAPTER 8

In his nonprofessional, private life, Russell pursued the love of hunting that had been instilled by his father when they lived in Montana. He typically hunted deer and elk in Eastern Washington, Oregon, or British Columbia. He rented a freezer locker in Everett to store the meat that a hunting trip would yield. Usual hunting partners included his father, Richard, or his son, Dick. It seems that he was as successful in hunting as he was in business.

My mother recalls the meat rationing during World War II. None of her friends' families had meat, but my mother dined nightly on moose steaks and elk burgers. Her friends were both repelled and envious. My mother thought nothing of it, as it had always been that way. She had grown up on wild game and, in fact, rarely had meat from the grocery store or butcher.

Russell R. Bradley with a large moose taken on one of his hunting trips.

CHAPTER 9

Russell's interest in weekend getaways from the city was satisfied serially with three different retreats. First, the family owned a small, beachfront cottage at Possession Point on Whidbey Island in Puget Sound. Its distance from their Everett home was less than ten miles as the crow flies; however, part of this involved crossing the water of Puget Sound. As there were no ferries on that route at the time, the family would pack up clothes, food, and other provisions for a weekend stay on the island, and then catch a ride on the US Mail boat that crossed once daily from nearby Mukilteo to the south end of Whidbey Island. They had to sit out on the exposed deck for the crossing, and my mother recalls several trips in the rain during which the family huddled under a tarp. When they arrived, it was necessary to carry their possessions to the cottage. The distance was probably only a few hundred yards, but my mother, who was then a child, recalls it as being miles.

"The farm" replaced the Possession Point cottage. While living in Everett after 1935, Russell bought a 200-acre farm near Snohomish, one of the towns in which the family had previously lived. Half of the farm was cleared for growing crops; the remainder was left wooded. Russell had two log homes built on the property, one for family visits and the other for his own father's retirement. Richard Bradley not only retired there but also acted as the caretaker for the property. He died in 1940. According to my mother, the farm had domestic animals of every type, ranging from geese to goats, just for the enjoyment of the children. "The caretaker" took care of them.

Russell looked for ways to profit from the farm. As it had a stream flowing through it, he imagined farming trout in a man-made lake. Subsequently, the stream was dammed where it flowed through a low area. A moderately sized lake formed, but before the trout could be introduced, disaster struck. Some neighboring children blocked the dam's spillway, which regulated the height of the water. When the water level rose to the top, the dam washed out. The resultant tidal wave down the stream's channel damaged and nearly destroyed a county bridge. That was the end of fish farming.

Russell turned next to cultivation of cascara trees, the bark of which could be sold and processed for medicinal purposes. Cascara trees grow best on the edge of a forest. In order to increase the linear footage of forest "edge" available for cultivation, Russell had wide paths similar to logging trails bull-dozed through the forest portion of the farm, thereby increasing the forest edge manyfold. Small cascaras were planted along each side of the trails, and bark eventually was harvested, but it is not known whether the effort was profitable. When the breaks had been created in the woods, Russell went to Eastern Washington and bought four riding horses, one for each member of the family. My mother fondly remembers how often the four of them would ride the trails together. Her brother, my uncle, claims however, that his mother rode her horse once or twice at most.

"The beach" followed "the farm" as the Bradley family's weekend retreat. Russell bought waterfront property at the north end of Camano Island. Camano is about twenty miles long. It stretches in a north-south orientation in the saltwater of Puget Sound, with its southern tip approximately offshore from Everett, where the family lived. Camano offered the huge advantage that they did not need to ride the US Mail boat to get there. They simply drove north from Everett on old Highway 99, across the Snohomish River Bridge, across Smith Island, through a wooded portion of the Tulalip Indian reservation, and across some farmland to the town of Stanwood, a total of twenty miles. At Stanwood, they turned west and crossed over a bridge to the north end of Camano Island. Since their beachfront property was at that end of the island and relatively close to the bridge, the commute was only thirty or forty minutes. This allowed them to come and go as they wished and carry their possessions to their property in their automobile.

This part of Camano Island offered some other invaluable advantages. The salmon fishing along the shore was outstanding, and a seemingly endless supply of clams was available for harvest at low tide. In addition, by placing a baited trap, similar to a lobster pot, just offshore overnight, they easily caught Dungeness crabs. Ecosystems change with time, however, especially when man interjects himself into the equation. Today, the salmon run is almost nonexistent and littleneck butter clams are found only rarely. Dungeness crab continues to be plentiful, and it is not uncommon for everyone fishing them to catch his daily limit of five crabs, especially just after the start of the season when crab numbers are greatest. The Skagit River enters this area of Puget Sound from the northeast and deposits silt, making the bay relatively shallow. This is apparently an optimal habitat for the growth of Dungeness crab, and the area is known as a Dungeness crab nursery in recognition of its prolific production of the delicious crustaceans.

In the century prior to Russell's purchase of property, there was a busy port at the north end of Camano Island for those seeking long, straight spars from first-growth forest to use as masts on sailing ships. A community had grown up there in the 1800s to supply what some considered to be the best spars available in the world. When steam-powered ships replaced those powered by wind, the demand for tall masts dropped, and the community dwindled away. A century later, in the mid-1900s, the area was being promoted and lots sold for recreational purposes. Some vestiges of the prior inhabitation remained, including a road along the bay and some old pilings protruding from the sand-and-gravel beach that had supported docks and piers.

The Puget Mill Company was selling waterfront lots for recreational development for $750 in 1938. The lot listed in the advertisement shown included fifty linear feet of waterfront, or $15 per front foot, as the pricing worked out. Russell reportedly bought his lot, which had sixty feet of frontage, in a prime location in the center of a bay for $2 per linear foot because the old logging road ran too close to the beach at that point to allow construction on the water side. Once he had a deed in hand, Russell petitioned the county to move that portion of the road an additional fifteen feet away from the beach to allow landowners on the water side to build homes on their lots. The county approved his petition, took fifteen feet from landowners on the other side, and moved the road inland, undoubtedly increasing the property's worth to the market value reflected in the advertisement.

A 1938 advertisement for waterfront land on Utsalady Bay, Camano Island, for recreational use.

CHAPTER 10

During their marriage, Russell and Helen had taken their two children on family vacations to such places as New York; California; Glacier National Park; and Kalispell, Montana; where Russell was born and lived to the age of eighteen. Russell had been impressed with the majestic Glacier National Park Lodge during its construction, while he was in junior high school in nearby Kalispell. The hotel site was purchased from the Piegan, a tribe of the Blackfoot Nation. The most famous and spectacular portion of the lodge contains the lobby and the dining room. It was built in 1912-1913 and opened to guests in the summer of 1913. The opening was a huge celebration attended by 600 invited guests and hundreds of Blackfoot Indians, who pitched teepees on the grounds. The Indians were said to have marveled at the ability of the white man to erect such a structure. The sixty immense timbers supporting the lodge are estimated to have been 500 to 800 years old when harvested. Each is forty feet long and thirty-six to forty-two inches in diameter. The timbers supporting the veranda are cedar logs from Washington State.

Helen and Russell admired the Lodge further during trips back to Glacier. When it came time to select a theme for the design of their new waterfront home on Camano Island, they chose to model it after the Lodge at Glacier National Park.

The house was built in 1946 and1947 on a three-foot-thick, concrete foundation laid over thirty feet of the sixty-foot frontage of their lot. It was built of logs in the style of the Glacier Park Lodge. Since half of the 200-acre farm near Snohomish was wooded, they had a ready source of building materials. A massive granite wall was erected through the center of the house, encompassing a large stone fireplace and chimney. Archways in the rock wall formed the entrances to the kitchen and the hallway to the bedroom and bathroom. A split-log staircase led to a large loft, providing sleeping space upstairs for guests or grandchildren. The main floor featured large bay windows across the entire western-facing front of the house, through which one could watch waves crash on the beach on a stormy day and see the summer sun set over the water each night. A six-foot diameter ship's wheel hung on a massive brass chain from the center beam of the ceiling. From the wheel were suspended seven old ship's lights, comprising a nautical chandelier to light the main room. The wheel came from a steam-powered paddle-wheeled tugboat that once plied the waters of the nearby Skagit River. The boat's captain was a good friend of Russell's and gave him the wheel when the boat was decommissioned.

The granite for the wall and fireplace came from a quarry adjacent to a nearby waterfall, appropriately named Granite Falls. Versions of the story differ, but the most likely is that Russell and his teenage son would go out to the quarry when it was closed on the weekends and use dynamite to blast out pieces of granite that they then loaded on a truck and drove to their construction site on Camano. The original blueprint building diagrams for the cabin still exist, and the granite-procurement legend is supported by a shopping list written in pencil on the back of one sheet. The list includes sticks of dynamite, fuse, and blasting caps.

Building the "beach house" in 1946. The Glacier National Park
Lodge in Montana influenced the log construction.

CHAPTER 11

Up until the time Russell constructed his log cabin on Camano, every house along his beach had its own private well for water. There were problems with salty seawater seeping into wells dug too close to the beach. There was also the potential for fecal coliform bacterial contamination if a well was dug too close to a neighbor's septic drain field, as was certainly possible on the relatively small building lots being sold. Russell helped solve the problem for himself and many others. He purchased another lot of land high up on the forested hillside that runs parallel to the beach, approximately a hundred yards back from the water's edge. Russell then donated the land to the community for the purpose of a shared water supply. A large well was dug on the site and a water storage tank installed. The hillside location provided sufficient elevation to guarantee a stable pressure head at the tap. Shares were then sold in the new water system, each valid for connection of one house. The number of shares was limited to the number of houses that the predicted well capacity could support. A flat annual fee for water was charged to those connected. Two additional wells were eventually constructed, more tanks added, and the New Utsalady Water System was born. Water is still provided in an unlimited amount for one flat annual fee (currently $400 per year).

Donna Shroyer has lived near the beach since she was born in 1934. She recalls the Bradley cabin being built when she was about thirteen years old. She remembers the magnificence of the structure as it went up. All of the nearby residents were impressed, as everything built previously had been along the lines of a cottage or fishing shack. Everyone liked the amiable Russell and many were proud that this popular Everett doctor had chosen to build such a high-quality house along their beach.

As noted, the house occupied approximately half of the sixty-foot frontage. When the house was completed, a thirty-foot-by-thirty-foot concrete patio was poured adjacent to the home entrance, and a massive custom canvas awning was sewn to suspend over the patio for protection from sun or rain. Square dances were frequently convened on the patio, which was a natural place for entertaining. Russell and Helen also threw annual summertime parties there for several of the Everett fraternal organizations to which Russell belonged.

The "beach house" remains in our family. Accompanying photographs show that it remains remarkably similar to when it was completed in 1947. On the wall still hang framed prints of Blackfoot Indians, cut from Great Northern promotional calendars decades ago. The individuals pictured are reportedly the Native Americans that my great-grandfather, Richard, knew or met while working as a ranger in Glacier National Park from 1910-1918. Since the railroad started using Blackfoot images on calendars in 1928, and Richard lived another decade beyond that time, it is likely that he was the one who collected the specific prints that are pictured in the home. They include images of Ales Eagle Plume, Many Mules, Homegun, Tough Bread, Morning Bird, Chief Eagle Calf, Dog Talking Gun, Chief Two Guns White Calf, and White Dog.

The "beach house" shortly after completion in 1947.

The "beach house" 2011.

CHAPTER 12

Russell's generosity to his family did not end with provision of a weekend retreat or elk burgers. The following letter written by Russell to his daughter Mary Lou, then an undergraduate at the University of Washington in Seattle exemplifies this.

Dear Mary Lou,

I guess our plans are just about complete for heading for little ol' New York.

We will go by United Air Lines Stratacruiser, leaving here Monday, June 19th about 11 P.M. and getting in New York Tuesday about 10 A.M.

We are getting Dick his car in Detroit, Michigan. We will stay in New York about a week and fly to Detroit, spend one day there so Dick can drive his car, then he and I will fly home, and you and Mother will drive the new car and visit on family the way. Won't that be fun?

We just heard Walter and C have sold the service station.

We had a poker party last night with the Wylands, Helen McArthur and a couple named Christianson's. Helen and I did not do so good. I lost $2.80 and I think Helen about $1.50. We had a good time and set our clocks ahead 1 hour about 2:30 and called it a night.

We have rented the Beach for one month to O'Donnas (Friedlanders manager) Tommie and Noel.

What color do you think the new car should be? All one color or a two-tone job?

Am sending you earrings. They look real nice.

Love,
Dad

CHAPTER 13

Russell's widely recognized demon was alcohol. My mother and her brother have both labeled their father as an alcoholic. When pressed to describe his typical actions in this regard, they note that Russell could apparently go long periods at a time without touching a drop of alcohol, be completely sober, work hard, achieve great things, and be loved by all. But if he had one sip of alcohol, he was reportedly unable to stop himself from drinking more. He would drop out of sight for a few days, only to return home days later professing not to know where he had been.

These absences, the frequency of which is debated, infuriated his wife, Helen. When people asked, she did not know where her husband was and did not know how to reply. Upon Russell's nocturnal return from one such surprise absence, son Dick was lying in bed and could hear his parents shouting. He heard his father shout at his mother, "Put that gun away!" underscoring Helen's frustration with the situation. During Russell's absences, office staff called scheduled patients and cancelled their appointments, saying that the doctor was "ill." When Russell would unexpectedly resurface, the cancelled patients were called and rescheduled on his first day back to work, and life rapidly returned to normal.

While this pattern of alcohol consumption meets the definition of binge drinking, Russell seems to have escaped the typical sequelae of binge drinking, at least up until the time of his death. The disorder is well known to be associated with poor job performance, something he is never described as having. It seems surprising that he could return to work after days of drinking and successfully see all the patients in a double- or triple-booked schedule on the first day, much less maintain the busiest practice in the state. Brain injury is more common with binge drinking as compared to alcohol consumption on a regular basis. It is marked by reduced executive function, including impaired planning function and memory. Since Russell appears to have been a binge alcoholic, perhaps these effects would have manifest with time. The possibility should at least be considered that he could have been doing something else during some of these periods of absence—something that he wanted to hide badly enough that he was even more willing to be seen as a binge alcoholic. It is unlikely that we will ever know for certain.

However, since it was alcohol that led to his ride from the bar with Harold Glenn Chase on the night of December 11, 1950, it truly was his biggest demon in the end.

CHAPTER 14

The small town of Darrington, Washington, lies in the foothills of the Cascade Mountains, about fifty northeast of Everett, Washington. The Sauk-Suiattle tribe was the first to settle in the mountain valley where Darrington now sits, attracted by the fertile soils of the valley floor and the abundant salmon runs in the Sauk and Stillaguamish Rivers. Miners from the East followed the Native Americans, seeking gold from the same rivers. Later, loggers came to harvest the dense forests of fir and cedar. The town grew up around the timber industry.

Darrington's current population is approximately 1,500 residents. Despite considerable contraction of the timber industry, small logging and lumber companies continue to provide the majority of jobs. The town is promoting recreation to bolster the economy, appealing to those interested in mountaineering, hiking, and river rafting.

On August 30, 1951, A. B. Wheeler, Darrington's mayor, called a special meeting of the town council to deal with the recent resignation of the town's police marshal. Town Council minutes from that meeting note that a Mr. Chase of Everett had applied for the position, requesting $325 per month and offering to furnish his own car if the city paid for gas, oil, and repairs.

Noting that "since it is impossible to obtain a qualified man to serve as marshal for any monies less than $325.00 per month," the Town Council agreed that the town would have to pay the amount and Mr. Chase was appointed marshal and street superintendant for Darrington. Council meeting minutes contain no information on what constituted "a qualified man." The Council requested that Chase begin work September 1, but he claimed to need time to appear in court as a witness. His job officially became effective September 5.

Mr. Harold G. Chase was twenty-two years old. He had served in the military and with the Snohomish County Sheriff's Posse. He had gotten some publicity for an attempted river rescue. He was a large man, approximately six-foot-one and weighed 220 to 240 pounds. Joyce Jones, a longtime Darrington resident and past mayor, was seventeen years old at the time Chase was hired. She recalls feeling uncomfortable in the presence of Mr. Chase, saying, "The hairs on the back of my neck stood up whenever I saw him." Joyce worked at the town's King Tut movie theater, selling tickets. Joyce's friend, Bob Ensley, also worked at the theater, selling popcorn and running the movie projector. When the new marshal was hired, Joyce's employer suggested that it would be safer for her to ride home with him when the theater closed late at night than to walk home alone. She recalls that her instinctive dislike of Chase precluded any thought of riding in a car with him. When the theater closed at night, she would peek out the door to make certain that he was not in sight and then run home by back alleys as fast as she could to avoid him.

On the afternoon of Saturday, September 8, 1951, Darrington resident Kathleen Robinson was home for the weekend from Seattle University. She sat at the drug store's ice cream fountain counter, talking to her friend, Donna. The new marshal sat silently nearby at the counter. Having experienced life in the big city, Kathleen remembers remarking to her friend, "This town is so boring. I wish someone would burn it down."

That evening, Joyce and Bob were working at the theater and noticed the new marshal making three trips behind the screen to the area where the stove and cleaning supplies were located. They discussed it and felt that it was a bit unusual, but dismissed the activity as something likely related to security. They locked up the theater as usual at the end of the night.

At around 4:00 a.m., the wailing of the town fire siren awakened Darrington residents. Joyce looked out her window and saw the sky glowing orange. She got dressed and walked in the direction of the fire, only to find the entire city block containing the theater ablaze. The marshal was helping to fight the fire and is said to have worked harder than anyone else did. Despite the efforts of fire fighters and citizens, the buildings on the block burned to the ground. Lost were the theater, the Red Top Tavern, a barbershop, and a shoe-repair store. A photograph in the January 9, 1952, edition of the *Seattle Post-Intelligencer* newspaper shows a uniformed Chase at the scene after the arrival of daylight, standing next to a fire truck and gazing at the pile of smoking wreckage.

An investigation of the fire ensued, and Chase's unusual activity in the theater that evening was revealed, as well as some other observations that cast suspicion on him. He was thought to be a likely arson suspect only four days after starting his job as marshal. Chase resigned the position in Darrington on September 10, 1951, but denied the charges. On September 19, local and regional law officials spoke with Chase and his father until 11:00 p.m. about the Darrington fire. At the end of the evening, a "truth serum" (sodium pentothal) interview of Chase was proposed and scheduled for the near future.

Of the businesses lost in the fire, only the Red Top Tavern was rebuilt, this time of brick. Kathleen Robinson has wondered ever since that day whether Chase overheard her remarks at the soda fountain, and if they somehow prompted him to set the fire.

The morning after the Darrington fire. The arrow points to Chase (in uniform). Photo entitled "Arson" from *Seattle Post-Intelligencer.*

Joyce Jones, former Darrington mayor, stands in front of the Red Top Tavern, the only building rebuilt after Harold Chase burned down the businesses on the block in 1951. The empty lot past the tavern is the former location of the King Tut Theater, where Joyce worked as a teenager and met Chase. (This photo was taken in 2012.)

CHAPTER 15

hase was not keen on the idea of a "truth serum" interview and disappeared after the meeting the same night that it was discussed. When Chase left town, he headed south to San Francisco. "I intended to keep going to Los Angeles, and into Mexico, but I ran out of money." Chase spent about six weeks in San Francisco until he was arrested November 29, 1951, on a Snohomish County warrant after applying for a government shipyard job. Undersheriff Earl "Buck" Weaver and Civil Deputy Sheriff Ed O. Walker accompanied him back to Everett. While in Portland en route, he signed a statement confessing to setting the Darrington fire, which had resulted in $40,000 in damages.

Upon arrival in Everett, Chase was booked into the Snohomish County jail on charges of first-degree arson for setting the Darrington fire. At arraignment, however, Chase pleaded "not guilty of the crime charged by reason of his insanity or mental irresponsibility at the time of the alleged commission of the crime charged" and "that said insanity or mental irresponsibility still exists."

On January 4, 1952, while waiting for a January 22 trial date on the arson charge, Chase attempted a jailbreak after learning the severity of sentences handed down to other prisoners that day. He convinced sixty-five-year-old

Deputy Sheriff Ingvald "Ink" Hoyland, the jailer, to unlock his cell so that he could open a window for ventilation. Once out of his cell, Chase attempted to overpower Hoyland. Chase attacked him with an improvised weapon made from a steel plate from the instep of another inmate's shoe attached to the end of a piece of broomstick. The weapon resembled a tomahawk. Hoyland suffered lacerations on his face and hands, but the jailbreak attempt was foiled when a jail trustee informed Chief Criminal Deputy Robert Lawe of the incident, and Chase was subdued. During the questioning that followed, Snohomish County Sheriff Warnock asked Chase if he realized that he might have killed the jailer. Chase is reported to have said, "It wouldn't have made any difference. I don't hate Ink. I just had to get out of there."

After he was questioned about the attempted breakout, Chase asked to speak with Sheriff Warnock. Warnock said that Chase told him "his conscience was bothering him and he wanted to clear his mind." Chase went on to tell an unbelievably fantastic story that included the statement that he had committed multiple murders. Prosecuting Attorney Phillip Sheridan and a deputy from his office were summoned, and Chase retold the story before a court recorder, who transcribed it in shorthand. Warnock said that there was no material difference between the two tellings, some details being added and some clarified under further questioning. The prosecuting attorney said that at no time were they able to shake Chase from the facts he told the first time. The following account was copied from public record.

Transcript of interview with Harold Glenn Chase taken in the presence of Tom Warnock, Phil Sheridan, John Walsh, Mr. McQuillen, and Norma Willett (stenographer).

January 5, 1952
1:00 a.m.

Sheridan: Your name is Harold Chase?

Chase: Yes, Harold Glenn Chase.

Sheridan: How old are you?

Chase: 22.

Sheridan: Now Harold, you are willing to talk to the Sheriff and myself and Mr. Walsh, he is from my office—you are willing to talk to the Sheriff and myself and Mr. Walsh, in the presence of Mr. McQuilln who represents the Everett Herald. You are also willing to talk to us with the complete understanding that you have an attorney who has been appointed by the Superior Court of Snohomish County. Judge Denney appointed Mr. Nellmeyer, a member of the Snohomish County bar, to represent you in the arson case. Is that right? With the full realization of what I just mentioned to you are you willing to talk on this new situation that has arisen where you admit your responsibility on an assault upon Mr. Hoyland who is the jailer for Snohomish County Jail? This assault was made on him on the evening of January 4, 1952, at 9:00 p.m. You are still willing to talk to us about that situation and any other questions that may be asked of you?

Chase: Yes.

Sheridan: Although you have counsel Mr. Hollmeyer who was assigned to represent you by the Superior Court of Snohomish County, you are willing to talk?

Chase: Yes.

Sheridan: Freely and voluntarily?

Chase: Yes.

Sheridan: No one ever threatened you?

Chase: No.

Sheridan: No one ever intimidated you?

Chase: No.

Sheridan: We are now talking to you at 1:00 a.m. on January 5, 1952, is that right?

Chase: Yes.

Sheridan: Is there something about the hour that we are talking to you which would indicate through any reason of fatigue or the fact that you are tired or that you are sleepy?

Chase: No, I am not sleepy.

Sheridan: That you aren't fully aware?

A: I thought about talking about it for a long time. I wanted to get it off my chest but didn't have the guts to do it.

Q: We are talking to you at 1:00 o'clock in the morning on January 5, 1952 and you are not being deprived of anything that would compel you to talk?

A: No.

Q: O.K. Now prior to Miss Willett's arrival here you had begun to tell us about Dr. Bradley?

A: Yes.

Q: Start from the beginning. I understand you made another statement in my absence to the Sheriff about what occurred on the evening of January 4, 1952. Now we are going to talk about Dr. Bradley.

A: Well, as I said before I met Dr. Bradley at the Monte Cristo Hotel. I was having a few drinks when he sat down next to me.

Hotel Monte Cristo, Everett, Washington. Location where
Harold Chase met Dr. R. R. Bradley in the bar.

Q: Can you recall the date?

A: No.

Q: Approximately how long ago was it?

A: I can't think. It was on a Friday night. No, it was in the middle of the week.

Q: Where were you working then?

A: I was working for my dad then.

Q: Can you remember how you knew it was Dr. Bradley? Did he introduce himself?

A: No, nobody introduced him. I didn't know who he was till after it was all over with. Somebody said something about doctor. They said doctor was getting pretty drunk.

Q: Were you alone?

A: Yes. I met him in there. I started having a few drinks. We started telling stories. The evening wore along. We were trying to pick up something.

Q: Were you trying to pick up some young ladies?

A: Yes. As the evening wore on he started talking about going someplace else. I figured, ah, heck, I don't have the money. Then he cashed a check. We passed a few jokes back and forth.

Q: How much was the check for?

A: $20.00 check. He pulled out a roll of bills that was in his pocket. There was $538.00.

Q: How did you know the exact amount?

A: I counted it afterwards, after I took it off him. Anyway he showed me the money after he cashed the check. He bought a few drinks. I was just about broke. I was feeling pretty good. He said, let's go over to Marysville. That was about 1:00 o'clock. I had the bartender help me take him out and put him in the car. He got in the pick-up and started going towards Marysville.

Walsh: He said that he wanted to go to Marysville?

Chase: Yes. He went to sleep sitting next to me. I thought about taking the money off him then.

Sheridan: Did you drive his car away?

Chase: No, I was in my own pick-up.

Warnock: Describe the pick-up for Mr. Sheridan.

Chase: It's a '42 Chev pickup.

Marshall: Did he indicate to you when you departed from the Monte Cristo that he had a car in the immediate vicinity?

Chase: He said he had a car around but would rather that I drive.

Sheridan: By the Monte Cristo you mean the Monte Cristo Hotel in Everett?

Chase: Yes. I started driving along. He was sitting next to me. I started thinking about the money, how I could sure use it. I turned off the road to the right over the bridge going towards the slaughterhouse. I stopped there and I started to take the money off him. I thought in my mind whether he would remember me. He was asleep and then he would wake up and jabber a little bit. He started putting up a fight. It was too late then. Anyway, I got out of the pick-up and walked around to the other side and took out a handkerchief and opened the door on that side and took the handkerchief and folded it up so it was just about yea big.

Walsh: About two inches square?

Chase: I folded it up so it was like that and took it in my hand like that.

Warnock: Why did you do that?

Chase: Not to make any bruises. He was sitting in the pick-up and I reached over on the left side right under the left here.

54

Warnock: Where did you learn that?

Chase: I learned it in the Army.

Sheridan: Whereabouts in the Army?

Chase: Aberdeen, Ft Mead.

Sheridan: What organization were you a member of?

Chase: I was a member of the ordinance. After we got in basic I got up with the sergeant. He started teaching me judo.

Sheridan: Was that in basic training?

Chase: No.

Sheridan: What was the sergeant's name?

Chase: He was with K company.

Walsh: Do you know what ordinance group, what serial number?

Chase: It was the group I took my basic with.

Walsh: Did he have a nickname?

Chase: Just called him sarge. There was another kid. He was a paratrooper.

Walsh: What was his name?

Chase: Tex.

Sheridan: What year was that?

Chase: 1947, I think.

Sheridan: At Camp Mead, Aberdeen Proving Grounds?

Chase: Yes.

Sheridan: Were you drafted?

Chase: I enlisted, when I was seventeen years old.

Sheridan: How long were you in the Army when you started receiving that training from that particular sergeant?

Chase: A month and a half. He was a master sergeant, no, a staff sergeant. I got books on judo and studied it.

Sheridan: Was that first aid treatment?

Chase: No.

Sheridan: When he was showing you that was a judo trick?

Chase: Judo, how to kill a man through bare hands.

Sheridan: Was that training for you?

Chase: Infantry combat training.

Sheridan: When the sergeant demonstrated it to you did he demonstrate it to you and you were a member?

Chase: He demonstrated it to a group but I got as he told me more.

Sheridan: You utilized that training on Dr. Bradley?

Chase: Yes.

Smith Island, Washington. First right turn after crossing the
Snohomish River Bridge en route from Everett to Marysville.
Site where Harold Chase strangled Dr. R. R. Bradley.

Sheridan: Over the packing house road, the first road north of the Snohomish Bridge on Highway 99 going to the right after you cross the bridge?

Chase: Yes.

Walsh: You told us when you were thinking about the money and you thought you would take it from him he started waking up?

Chase: It hit me in my mind that he might remember me. I just meant to knock him out. I lost control.

Walsh: You started to apply the pressure and thought you might as well go ahead with it?

Chase: No, I can't explain it. I started to apply the pressure and didn't want to give up.

Walsh: Have you tried it before?

Chase: Yes, I used it before.

Walsh: To cause someone's death?

Chase: Yes.

Walsh: And you knew it would result in death?

Chase: Yes.

Walsh: You started to apply the pressure and kept right on going?

Chase: Yes.

Sheridan: Referring back to the Monte Cristo Hotel, how long had you been drinking before you met Dr. Bradley?

Chase: Possibly a couple of hours.

Sheridan: What had you been drinking?

Chase: I don't know exactly. I had been sitting at the bar.

Sheridan: Did you make the acquaintance of Dr. Bradley at the bar?

Chase: Yes, he sat down next to me at the bar.

Sheridan: You discussed the possibility of picking up some female companions?

Chase: Yes.

Sheridan: He cashed a check?

Chase: Yes,

Sheridan: For $20.00?

Chase: Yes.

Sheridan: A moment or two later you noticed he had a roll on him?

Chase: He didn't want them to know about it at the Monte Cristo.

Sheridan: What were the denominations of bills?

Chase: There were some twenties, some tens, some fives, and a few ones, I don't know exactly.

Walsh: I would like to know if you remember the bartender that was working there.

Chase: I think it was Brownlee. There is one girl waitress that would remember me.

Warnock: Is that Pauline?

Chase: Yes.

Warnock: Did Brownlee cash the check?

Chase: Yes.

Sheridan: Before the sheriff asked you the last question you momentarily paused to take a drink. What were you drinking?

Chase: Water.

Sheridan: Given to you by the Sheriff?

Chase: Yes.

Warnock: From the time you said you got out on the driver's side you said you went over to the passenger's side?

Chase: Yes. A car went by. It was an old beat-up Ford. I ducked behind the door.

Warnock: You did go around the passenger's side and took the handkerchief and folded it?

Chase: Yes.

Warnock: Did he stir then?

Chase: Not until I applied the pressure.

Walsh: How long do you think it took to kill him?

Chase: Absolutely to kill him it took about two minutes, two or three.

Walsh: What was the sensation, was there some relaxation in the body?

Chase: He struggled a little bit, relaxed, his bowels started to move.

Sheridan: How did you know that?

Chase: There was an odor.

Sheridan: Did you masturbate at that time?

Chase: No.

Sheridan: Did you get sexual pleasure?

Chase: No.

Walsh: Why did you use your handkerchief instead of your hand?

Chase: Not to leave a bruise.

Sheridan: Where did you get that training?

Chase: I just read about it.

Sheridan: There wasn't any bruising?

Chase: No.

Warnock: Then what did you do?

Chase: I took the money out of his pocket. He had a billfold, one of those secretaries. He had two of them. He had one pocket wallet and a secretary. He had one wallet in his back pocket and one in his inside pocket.

Sheridan: Which one had money in it?

Chase: The one up here in his inside coat pocket.

Sheridan: I asked you a little while ago and I merely ask you due to the fact that I know about your mental temperament and also based on the story you wrote which we still have in our office.

Chase: I would like to get everything straightened out if I possibly could.

Sheridan: Before you get that straight, it is my observation that people do things like you say you have done to get some sexual pleasure. Did you get sexual pleasure?

Chase: No, I just felt relaxed, felt good.

Sheridan: Yes, full of pep?

Chase: Yes, I felt good, like I was relieved of something that was building up in my mind, something like that.

Sheridan: Now to get this straight, what was your first thought after you saw Dr. Bradley was dead?

Chase: I got scared, didn't know what to do with the body. I decided I would take him to the hospital. For some reason it came to my mind he could have had a heart attack.

Warnock: Right from the time you knew he was dead take us through the story of what you did where you went.

Chase: I reached in his pocket and pulled out his billfold and grabbed it and stuck it in my own pocket. I really didn't realize he was dead until his bowels started to move and the odor hit me. I thought about leaving him right there, I put the handkerchief back in the pocket and went around to the other side of the car. I got into the car, drove down to the packing plant, turned around and drove straight to the hospital.

Sheridan: Which hospital?

Chase: General. I got out of the car, ran in and asked for adrenalin. Then I went back to the car. Then the nurse came out. I said it's too late. She grabbed ahold of his wrist. She was monkeying with him. I ran in and called the Sheriff's office and waited for 5 or 10 minutes and Clarence DeMars and Larraine came in their car and a little while later I told Clarence DeMars and Larraine that after I left the Monte Cristo Hotel I was going to take him home, this waitress told me his address on Grand someplace. I think I told him I lost the way and was driving around and he had a heart attack.

Walsh: You stayed in the hospital until the Sheriff's office came?

Chase: Yes.

Warnock: You said you took him home and thought he had a heart attack on the way home and went back to the hospital?

Chase: Yes.

Sheridan: In order to eliminate any suspicion that he had been robbed, did you leave any money on him?

Chase: $2.00.

Sheridan: That was what was left in his pocket?

Chase: I left him what was left out of the check he cashed.

Sheridan: Have you made a study of these types of deaths?

Chase: Well, at the time I was in the service I made a study of different types of death, how to kill a person.

Sheridan: You believed the doctor was dead because of the release of his bowels?

Chase: Yes.

Sheridan: Did you have any training in that respect before?

Chase: I learned that when I was transferred to the medical corps.

Sheridan: Ever taken care of dead people?

Chase: I seen them die in the hospital.

Sheridan: But they normally don't have a release of the bowels?

Chase: No.

Sheridan: I mean if any one of us six here would have a heart attack that we would have relaxation of the bowels?

Chase: It would be a little bit after.

Sheridan: Where did you get your training?

Chase: At Percy Jones General Hospital. I was a patient for two months. Then I transferred into the medical orderly in the ward.

Sheridan: What I am driving at it this. You were confident that if anyone examined him, anyone familiar in medical training would readily discern that he had had a heart attack.

Sheridan: Are you making this statement for the purpose of creating some sort of hero worship?

Chase: No, I am not.

Walsh: I would like to ask this. You and I talked here before about the first degree arson matter. You expressed a willingness that you wanted to plead guilty on arson and go to the State Penitentiary for some sort of psychiatric care. Was your willingness to pay for the charge a reason for your wanting to avoid trial and avoid publicity on the arson charge. Did that occur to you at any time?

Chase: No.

Walsh: We were talking when Weaver was here and the two people from the fire investigator's office and Mr. Holmquist was here. Were you thinking at all at that time about Bradley's death?

Chase: No.

Walsh: Nothing about Bradley occurred to you?

Chase: No.

Walsh: When did this thing begin to work on you at night?

Chase: I would lay and think about it. The first thing I would know I would wake up in a cold sweat.

Warnock: You said cold sweats bothered you in Sedro Woolley?

Chase: I was thinking about Sedro Woolley.

Warnock: What was his name?

Chase: I really don't know.

Warnock: Was he an inmate?

Chase: Yes.

Warnock: When was this?

Chase: I was up there. I got the keys to the restraining belts. I was helping out.

Warnock: What ward was that in?

Chase: The one I was in.

Warnock: Which ward were you in?

Chase: I don't know which ward it was.

Warnock: How old a man was he?

Chase: About forty-five.

Warnock: You say this happened while you were there?

Chase: Yes.

Warnock: How long after you were there?

Chase: About a month. This patient he went around there—he was in a restraining belt. He was giving me a hard time, calling me names, sassing me. He would mope around.

Walsh: Would you go around by yourself?

Chase: No, he would come in and sit down next to you and stare at you. I got sore. I was about ready to blow my top. This is the first time in my life it entered my mind to kill somebody.

Walsh: Was he the first person you killed?

Chase: Yes.

Warnock: Did you tell anyone up there he was getting on your nerves?

Chase: Yes.

Warnock: Who did you tell?

Chase: Goad, one of the orderlies.

Warnock: Then what happened from then on?

Chase: Well, as long as I am going to do it I might as well draw a little diagram for you here. I went in and didn't bother with the handkerchief. I took my hand and strangled him. I put both hands around the front of his neck. I loosened his restraining belt so it would look like he slipped out of it.

Walsh: About how old of a man was he?

Chase: About forty-five.

Walsh: Did he have any characteristics? White or black?

Chase: He was a white fellow.

Walsh: What did you call him?

Chase: I don't know.

Walsh: What color was his hair?

Chase: He was very bald.

Walsh: What color was his hair.

Chase: Dark gray.

Walsh: Did he have any beard?

Chase: He had a light beard at the time. He was kind of a heavy and short fellow.

Walsh: Did he have a great big nose or a great big mouth or any particular appearance?

Chase: No.

Walsh: Pimples on his face?

Chase: No.

Walsh: Any scars?

Chase: Not that I remember.

Warnock: Was there anybody else on the floor?

Chase: An orderly sitting in the office.

Warnock: What time of night was it?

Chase: Nine o'clock at night.

Warnock: Were any of the orderlys (sic) there?

Chase: Goad was the only one.

Warnock: Nobody else?

Chase: No.

Warnock: Was there any nurse around?

Chase: The nurses were out of the ward at the time. I went down and yelled and ran and picked him up, as if I was trying to take the pressure off. Goad got there and started giving artificial respiration.

Sheridan: What did you feel, relief?

Chase: I was sorry about it that time.

Walsh: You said you were sorry about it?

Chase: I don't know.

Walsh: Did you feel you did a good thing or a bad thing?

Chase: I felt bad. I didn't think about doing anything to the patient.

Walsh: Did you have a feeling about whether it was right or wrong?

Chase: No.

Walsh: What do you think about it now?

Chase: It kept bothering me. That's the reason I wanted to get it off my chest. I laid in there and wanted to get everything cleared off my mind.

Walsh: Do you believe in God?

Chase: Yes.

Walsh: Do you think it is wrong?

Chase: Yes.

Warnock: Did anybody examine you concerning the accident?

Chase: Yes, they questioned me. The policeman from Skagit County questioned me.

Warnock: Do you know his name?

Chase: No.

Warnock: What did he look like?

Chase: He was a rather tall young fellow.

Warnock: Was it the same evening this deputy sheriff came?

Chase: Yes.

Warnock: How long after that?

Chase: Around 12:00 o'clock.

Warnock: Where was the nurse in charge? Then was the nurse in charge?

Chase: Yes. I don't know the young doctor—one of the young internes (sic) up there came down and worked on the patient. After the doctor examined him he said it was accidental death. I felt better.

Warnock: You don't know the doctor's name?

Chase: No, I don't.

Sheridan: The doctor's diagnosis was accidental death (sic)?

Chase: For hanging, suicide.

Sheridan: How did he account for the bruises on the side of his face?

Chase: The bruises didn't come out then. They come out later.

Warnock: How do you know?

Chase: Because I helped clean him up—wrapping, tying and stuffing. You know, tie and then stuff with cotton so they won't make too much mess. I was helping. Goad was doing that.

Sheridan: There is only one thing not too clear in my mind. When you observed the patient he was prostrate on the floor?

Chase: No, he wasn't. He was lying on the bed.

Sheridan: You went up and choked him while he was laying in bed?

Chase: Yes.

Sheridan: He wasn't doing any harm to you?

Chase: No.

Walker: How long did you think about it?

Chase: Off and on for about a week.

Sheridan: Were you sleeping in the same room?

Chase: No.

Sheridan: How was Dr. Bradley dressed?

Chase: He had a blue suit on with little lines running through it. About like what Mr. Laws wears.

Sheridan: At any time did you pay your respects to the widow of Dr. Bradley?

Chase: Yes.

Sheridan: How soon afterwards?

Chase: That same evening.

Sheridan: Where at?

Chase: At her home. I asked Clarence if I could go along up to the house. Clarence told about the accident of her husband's death. I told her I tried to do everything I could to save her life.

Sheridan: Did you talk to Mrs. Bradley that evening?

Chase: Yes, she came out and said, I knew it was going to happen.

Sheridan: Did she say why?

Chase: No.

Sheridan: Did she say anything about him being a heavy drinker?

Chase: He was a very heavy drinker, she said herself.

Sheridan: Did he have glasses on that evening?

Chase: I don't remember.

Sheridan: You are pretty meticulous in details. It seems to me you might remember whether he had glasses on.

Chase: No, he didn't have glasses.

Sheridan: You had a good look at him at the Monte Cristo?

Chase: Yes.

Sheridan: You are sure he didn't have glasses on?

Chase: I think he had them on when he came into the Monte Cristo?

Sheridan: How long did you drink with him at the Monte Cristo?

Chase: About an hour and a half.

Warnock: Glenn, are we imposing on you by keeping you up so late? Just say the word if you want to go to bed into the cell to lay down.

Chase: I want to get everything off my chest.

Walker: You told me about your experience with Dr. Bradley the next morning?

Chase: Yes.

Walker: Where were you at?

Chase: I don't remember exactly.

Walker: You were in my car?

Chase: Yes.

Walker: You gave me all the details, how everything happened?

Chase: Yes.

Walker: The next day?

Chase: Yes.

Walker: If I remember correctly, you said that you didn't want to drink with him, you couldn't take it.

Chase: He was drinking quite a bit.

Sheridan: What did you do with the $538.00?

Chase: I went to Seattle down on First Avenue, went to different nightclubs and spent it, mostly at the Caballero. That's on Pike between 7th and 8th.

Sheridan: When did you spend it? How soon after the doctor's death?

Warnock: He means how long did the money last?

Chase: About a week.

Sheridan: Did you spend any money on the boys around here?

Chase: I did from the Casino.

Sheridan: In what way did you spend it out there?

Walker: Was that dollar bill part of the money you got from Dr. Bradley?

Chase: Yes.

Sheridan: I am going to ask you again, is this a cock and bull story?

Chase: No it isn't.

Walsh: I want to know, you told us you were being blackmailed on a deal. I want to know if Glenn might have told these folks at any time drinking about this deal with Dr. Bradley.

Chase: One person could verify all of it. Reno, right next to the Liberty Theater.

Sheridan: What kind of place is he in?

Chase: Mexican spaghetti joint.

Walsh: Did you tell him about Dr. Bradley?

Chase: No, I mentioned other things.

Sheridan: Let's get back to when you got involved with that girl.

Chase: I want to get it all cleared up.

Sheridan: We will see what we can do to get it cleared up. Remember the night we talked to you about the Darrington fire in the Sheriff's office in the presence of your father and Mr. Laws and Mr. Walsh and Vic Holmquist, the parole officer was present and I think two members of the Fire Marshal's office, one was Charlie Lander from the underwriters and Bruce Igou. When we questioned you about that we questioned you for the purpose of convincing your father you were doing a lot of things that weren't proper. I believe you said you were drunk when you performed that act in the motion picture.

Chase: No, I was hoppy (sic). I'd been smoking weeds.

Sheridan: Do you think under the influence of weeds that you told anybody about the man in Northern State Hospital in Sedro Woolley and the Dr. Bradley killing?

Chase: I don't know.

Sheridan: Let me ask you this. I don't want any cock and bull story. Did anybody try to blackmail you?

Chase: No.

Sheridan: No one tried to blackmail you about the picture?

Chase: No.

Sheridan: No one tried to blackmail you while you were under the influence of weeds?

Chase: No.

Warnock: How did you happen to be in Frisco?

Chase: I remember the night I came home, I sat around the house and started getting a little scared. I knew then if I went down and took the sodium pentothal test.

Sheridan: You are referring to the agreement you made in the presence of your father and myself and Mr. Walsh, Mr. Landis and Bruce

Igou. It was agreed that night in the presence of your father in order to clear up the Darrington fire that you would voluntarily submit to a sodium pentothal test examination before Dr. Stolzheise in Seattle who had previously examined you as a result of fires in the Pinehurst District, is that right?

Chase: Yes.

Sheridan: You were thinking about that when you went home, is that right?

Chase: Yes. I went around home and then I thought the heck with it. If I take off things will cool down a little bit and maybe I can hide out. I packed my clothes. My dad and mother tried to stop me. I got mad at mother and dad, called mother a few names so she would get mad and want me to leave. I left around 12:00 o'clock or a little after. Dad came out and opened the door and tried to stop me. I jerked the door and drove off. I drove into Seattle. I stopped at my sister's place and stayed there until early morning, drove out to Gail's place and said good-bye to her and drove to San Francisco.

Walsh: Was this your father's pick-up?

Chase: In my own Dodge. I got down there and was running short of money. I bumped into a few fellows at the Y, started going night clubbing. I started running out of money so there are a lot of queers running around, got the idea I would roll a few of them. Then I met a fellow at Rex's across from the Y.M.C.A. It's a tavern, cocktail lounge on Golden Gate Avenue.

Walsh: Is that a hangout for queers?

Chase: No.

Sheridan: Where do the queers hang out?

Chase: Down on Market and down on Third. I met Joe at Rex's. He was a tourist, just sight-seeing. We started talking. I said, come with me, I got a car. We started driving around. We drove to the amusement park, we kept driving, having fun, just sight-seeing. He was forking the bill, so we started driving along the highway that leads to the Cliff House. We parked and walked down on the beach for awhile. I thought I would like to have some money.

Walsh: How did you know he had any?

Chase: He was spending it on me for me taking him around and showing him the sights. He was forking most of the bill. We went down—round the amusement park and went out for a drive along the beach, parked and started walking along the beach for awhile. The sun started getting low. We drove on past the academy and turned to the right and you go on down by a lot of cliffs. We got out and watched the sun going down. We went back to the car and sat and talked and smoked a cigarette and I reached in the back seat and got a coke bottle. I conked him on the back of the head with the pop bottle. The glass is still in the car in the roof. In fact, it cut me up a little bit. I knocked him out, took his money, over $200.00, mostly $10.00 bills, closer to $300.00, threw him over the cliff and went back to San Francisco. I stopped at the gas station. Jerry said, "What happened to you"? I paid him for my past rent, Jerry Fagen his name is, went over to the Y, changed clothes and Frank, a kid at the Y, we went up to Chinatown, went to the Sky Room. That's the night I spent close to $150.00 up there drinking champagne and everything else.

Warnock: Was there much bleeding?

Chase: Yes, you can probably find a trace of it in the car.

Warnock: Did he die right away?

Chase: He was dead when I turned him over.

Sheridan: Did this man speak with a dialect?

Chase: Yes.

Sheridan: Did he ever tell you anything about his background?

Chase: He was a schoolteacher.

Sheridan: Where?

Chase: Someplace in France.

Sheridan: After you hit him with the pop bottle, what happened?

Chase: I walked around the car and took the money and threw him over my shoulder.

Warnock: Did you have an overcoat on?

Cliffs north of the old amusement park and original Chart House Restaurant in San Francisco, where Chase claimed to have thrown the body of the French tourist, Joe.

Walsh: You put him over your shoulder?

Chase: Yes.

Warnock: Give me a good physical description of this man.

Chase: He was about Mr. Sheridan's build, just about Mr. Sheridan's height. He was about 5'9" or 10." I would say he weighed 160 pounds. He was very skinny. He had a blue suit with marks running through the material. It was a dark colored suit.

Warnock: What about his hair?

Chase: It was black.

Sheridan: Did he wear glasses?

Chase: No; I would say he was 30 something.

Walsh: Did you notice if he had rings on?

Chase: No, I didn't pay any attention.

Warnock: Did he have on a topcoat?

Chase: No.

Warnock: What kind of hair?

Chase: Blackish brown. He had a brief case. I threw it in the trash bar-rel at the Y.M.C.A.

Warnock: Where was he living?

Chase: It was something square.

Chase: I had a light sport jacket on and you can check with the cleaners about his blood on it. She wanted to know how I got the blood on it.

Warnock: Was it on Market Street?

Chase: A little ways off Market Street.

Walsh: You put him over your shoulder?

Chase: Yes.

Walsh: And then what?

Chase: I walked up to the edge of the bank.

Walsh: How far did you have to walk?

Chase: I would say about 25, 30 feet.

Walsh: Was there a railing there?

Chase: There is a wall that goes up over the cliff and one goes down to a gully. There is a sign there that says, Danger undertow.

Warnock: That's out by the side of the cliff?

Chase: Yes.

Warnock: When you threw him over did you leave identification on him?

Chase: Yes. I just took his money.

Sheridan: What did he have is his brief case?

Chase: Just mostly school papers.

Sheridan: Could you read the papers?

Chase: No, I looked at them. I know something else. He wrote his name down in a little red book I have at home in his own handwriting. I was going to meet him later.

Walker: Did you take his wallet?

Chase: No.

Walker: What type of wallet was it? Would you call it a pocket secretary?

Chase: No, a wallet. I would say maybe 6 inches long. I really don't know.

Walker: What was the color of it?

Chase: Black.

Warnock: Did he have passport papers?

Chase: Yes.

Sheridan: What did the passport papers look like?

Chase: It had his picture on there with his name above. His passport was in a little folded book made out of leather.

Warnock: Was that in his wallet?

Chase: Yes, in his wallet.

Warnock: That remained on the body?

Chase: Yes.

Warnock: When we are asking you that question, it is now about 2:20 A.M. on the morning of January 5, 1952. Would you like to go on?

Chase: Yes.

Warnock: On the way home do you recall coming home with Ed Walker and Buck and do you recall being housed as a prisoner en route in Oregon?

Chase: Yes.

Warnock: Would you tell us what you had planned?

Chase: I don't know if it would ever work. It was just like a kid I will tell you that.

Walker: This is in the County Jail in Klamath Falls, Oregon.

Chase: Ed left me and I was sitting there pouting. I started figuring whether I could get out. I broke the top off the pipe going by the shower. I asked some of the guys running around, I said does the jailer ever come back. They said, once in awhile. I got the idea of tearing up blankets, wove a rope heavy enough to hold me, fixed it up to look like I hanged myself.

Walker: What did you have ready for him?

Chase: I think it was a mop handle. I had it stuck in my back pocket. I was going to hit him with that. I made a rumpus, there was no noise, nothing happened. I sat down and started smoking.

Warnock: Anything else you have done of a violent nature? Where someone might have been killed or hurt?

Chase: No.

Walker: Now the night before you were picked up in San Francisco what happened?

Chase: The queers were getting wise of fellows picking them up and rolling them. The next morning I borrowed $2.00 from the cleaning woman. I was working at the San Francisco Naval Yard. I was in the kitchen and started making myself some corn meal mush. I got so I was in charge of the television and recreation hall. Nobody else wanted it. If I wanted to watch a movie I could go in and turn it on. I sat in the kitchen reading the newspaper while my mush was cooking. I don't know to this day how it went off or anything. I know I got myself a little touch of gas. They believe I tried to commit suicide. I didn't. Somehow the flame went out. I don't know how, I was sitting reading the newspaper.

Sheridan: I want to ask a few things about San Francisco. How long were there (sic) altogether from the time you left here until you were picked up by members of the sheriff's office, Snohomish County?

Chase: I got there on Sunday. I checked in the Y the following Sunday. No, it was Wednesday night.

Warnock: Do you read the papers?

Chase: Not very much, why?

Warnock: Did you ever read an account of that murder?

Chase: No.

Walker: Did this man land in the water?

Chase. I don't know.

Walker: Was there water at the foot of the cliff?

Chase: Yes, right down.

Walker: What time of day was it?

Chase: Just at sundown.

Walker: How far was it from the playland that you tossed this man over?

Chase: About twenty years. (sic)

Walker: South or north?

Chase: You got me. You stop at a stop sign, turn to the right, go along the road 'til you get by the cliff, keep going, I don't know where you end up.

Sheridan: Did this Frenchman have a name?

Chase: Joe.

Sheridan: How long did you know him?

Chase: About 3 or 4 hours.

Sheridan: Where did you meet him? In a restaurant or tavern or what was it?

Chase: Rex's. An eating place and cocktail lounge.

Sheridan: What's the location again?

Chase: Right on Golden Gate Avenue.

Sheridan: What time of day did you first meet him?

Chase: Two o'clock in the afternoon.

Sheridan: How long did you remain with him at Rex's before you went down to the Golden Gate Bridge?

Chase: About an hour.

Sheridan: You went to California in a Dodge coupe?

Chase: Yes.

Sheridan: Were you behind the driver's seat when you assaulted this man?

Chase: Yes.

Sheridan: Right behind the steering wheel?

Chase: Yes.

Sheridan: Did it knock him unconscious?

Chase: Yes.

Sheridan: Was it empty?

Chase: No, full of pop.

Sheridan: In order for the Sheriff's office to get in touch with you, how did they locate you?

Chase: I went to work for a salvage company burning aluminum. I wasn't fast enough. I couldn't burn fast enough. I never done it before with a cutting torch. I worked four days with them. Then I played around for awhile and started robbing queers. I got tired of laying around and wanted a real job. I started looking around for other jobs. Jobs are not as easy to find as people think. I went out to Hunter's Point finally and got a job with the government at the San Francisco Naval Shipyard.

Sheridan: Who informed you as to where the queers hang out?

Chase: Some fellows at the Y.

Walker: Did you have any idea if this Joe was a queer?

Chase: I thought he was, I don't know.

Walker: How did you know?

Chase: He had a squeaky voice.

Sheridan: Did you have any illicit acts while down there, either male or female?

Chase: No.

Sheridan: How did you get in so solid at the Y?

Chase: I was watching the World Series one day. This kid was monkeying with it and couldn't get it to work. I walked up and grabbed a hold of the knobs and turned the aerial.

Sheridan: What time of day was that?

Chase: During the day, in the morning before noon when the World Series was on. I focused it in good.

Sheridan: Did you participate in any fire as an observer?

Chase: No.

Sheridan: Did the police interview you at the scene of a fire? It is my understanding that you were at a fire down there and interviewed by the police.

Chase: No.

Walker: You were interviewed by the police?

Chase: After I was picked up.

Sheridan: What fires were they?

Chase: Cars.

Sheridan: Automobiles or box cars?

Chase: Cars, automobiles.

Sheridan: You weren't interviewed at any fires where human lives were lost?

Chase: No.

Sheridan: You got into San Francisco on a Sunday. Do you remember if that was the same week you met Joe? Were you working at all?

Chase: I wasn't working at all.

Walsh: You already had lost your job burning aluminum but hadn't got the job at Hunter's Point?

Chase: No.

Walsh: What about the first or third week?

Chase: It was the third week.

Walsh: What day was it?

Chase: On Wednesday because it was on Wednesday night that I went up to the Sky Room. It was the same night and I spent so much money and got stupid drunk.

Sheridan: Was there anything you can recall that would indicate where he was living?

Chase: No.

Walker: It wouldn't be the Hotel Mark Hopkins?

Chase: That's it.

Warnock: Do you recall from the time you got here just about what you did? Would he be registered at the hotel?

Chase: I don't know. He said he had been there a couple of days. I went to work on Tuesday, got there on Sunday and worked there four days.

Warnock: You weren't fast enough so you got laid off?

Chase: Yes.

Warnock: For about 2 ½ weeks no work?

Chase: Yes.

Warnock: To get back to Dr. Bradley are you sure you didn't strangle him with your hands?

Chase: No.

Warnock: You are absolutely positive you didn't put your hands on his neck? Think hard. While you are thinking about that, I will ask you another question. Had Mrs. Bradley seen the body at the time you talked to her?

Chase: No.

Warnock: She hadn't seen it?

Chase: No, she hadn't.

Warnock: Can you remember, you didn't reach over and choke him with your hands? Now you did that at Sedro Woolley.

Chase: I think maybe I did. I don't know exactly.

Warnock: Could you have had your whole hand up there?

Chase: I probably did.

Warnock: Was he trying to move?

Chase: Yes.

Warnock: More than likely you don't think the pressure was made with the hand instead of using one finger?

Chase: I don't know if I did or not.

Warnock: What did you do with the other hand?

Chase: I was holding his.

Warnock: If you had this finger on the pressure point where would the rest of the hand be?

Chase: Laying across the head like this.

Sheridan: Did you choke Joe in San Francisco?

Chase: No.

Sheridan: Have you ever made any sadistic attacks on a woman?

Chase: I haven't touched a woman or hit a woman or anything like that.

Warnock: Let me ask you something else. Do you have any coercion in any way with men?

Chase: No.

Warnock: Have you had any? Was there anything like that proposed with Dr. Bradley?

Chase: He might have. I don't remember exactly.

Warnock: What do you mean, he might have? Did he have some relations with you?

Chase: I don't remember.

Warnock: This Joe fellow, was he a queer?

Chase: I think so.

Warnock: Have you engaged in any sodomy up in this tank?

Chase: No.

Sheridan: With regards to the inmates in Sedro Woolley, did you engage in any homosexual practice?

Chase: No, I didn't.

Sheridan: Did you want to?

Chase: No.

Sheridan: Did you practice self-abuse there?

Chase: Probably once or twice.

Sheridan: The Sheriff asked you about here in the tank. Did you hear any discussion in the tank? Did you know Kennedy?

Chase: I was in the lower tank.

Walsh: Maybe Glen (sic) can remember if he tries a little harder about the proposition made with Dr. Bradley.

Chase: Well, where we were heading was to a cat house in Marysville.

Walsh: What was the name of the cat house?

Chase: He mentioned it. It's on the main drag.

Walsh: Upstairs?

Chase: Upstairs.

Walsh: Was it over a tavern or what was it over?

Chase: He said he turned off a street and it was around the corner a little past the liquor store upstairs.

Sheridan: Have you been there?

Chase: No.

Sheridan: Did he say you could get a drink there?

Chase: He said we could get a drink.

Sheridan: Did he mention any woman's name?

Chase: He said let's go see Kay.

Sheridan: Did he say she ran the place?

Chase: I don't remember.

Sheridan: You mentioned about a Ford going by as you stopped. Did you stop on Highway 99?

Chase: On the road to the packing house.

Sheridan: You could see Highway 99. How far up the road were you?

Chase: About half a block.

Warnock: What is the description of the car that passed you?

Sheridan: I want to get the details about tonight. Did Dickinson help out in the deal tonight?

Chase: I think he did. I would like to get something else off my chest. You might as well write it on another piece of paper or is it all right to write it on the same one, relative to the Casino. I want to get it off my chest now. I was around the Casino quite often helping out as much as I possibly could. This guy was kidding me about having too much money in there. It was on Friday night. It was around between four and five in the morning. That night I was at the Casino for a while, then left and went to a movie at the Liberty Theatre in Seattle. I planned to do it before but I backed out. So I drove by and drove down the road and then turned around and came back and parked by the power plant and came there. I took a bag of tools and I had gloves and I had a hunting knife so I could peel the shingles. Then I drilled a series of holes around and sawed a hole in the side of the building. I got in and rushed to the ice box.

Sheridan: How did you know the money was in the ice box?

Chase: I knew that was where he kept it.

Sheridan: How did you know that?

Chase: I locked up and stayed around and guarded it while they closed up.

Warnock: Is that while you were working there?

Chase: I was a sheriff's deputy.

Warnock: Who was with you?

Chase: Nobody.

Warnock: What car did you have?

Chase: The pick-up.

Warnock: What was the time?

Chase: Between 4 and 5.

Warnock: How long do you figure it took you to get into the place and get the money and get out of there?

Chase: Maybe ten minutes. I wasn't in there over three minutes.

Sheridan: How much money did you get?

Chase: $1400.00.

Walsh: When about was this, in 1951?

Chase: In 1950.

Walsh: Before the Darrington deal?

Chase: Yes.

Walsh: Before the Silvana deal came up?

Chase: Yes.

Walsh: In the summer?

Chase: Yes.

Sheridan: You made this statement to us during the period of time which you are charged with first degree arson. This statement is given to us this evening. You are now finishing about 3 A.M. in the morning. This statement is made freely and voluntarily without any threats from the Prosecutor's Office or the Sheriff's Office?

Chase: Yes.

Sheridan: In other words you wanted to make this statement without having an attorney present?

Chase: I wanted to get it off my chest.

Sheridan: This interview is the result of an attack made on the jailor, Mr. Heilor?

Chase: Yes.

Sheridan: That was last night, January 4, 1952?

Chase: Yes.

Sheridan: You made this statement with the full realization that if corroborated it may be used against you?

Chase: Yes.

Sheridan: Was this not a figment of your imagination?

Chase: No.

Sheridan: From the standpoint of seeking notoriety with respect to your name?

Chase: No, it isn't.

Sheridan: You will make a statement under a lie detector or truth serum voluntarily now?

Chase: Yes.

Sheridan: If we obtain the services of a psychiatrist tomorrow you will be willing to submit to him?

Chase: Yes.

Sheridan: These statements that you give us are not made with the intention to obstruct or obscure the arson case pending against you or in other words, to lend some support to the fact that you might not be sane?

Chase: I haven't thought about that.

Sheridan: You knew what you were doing when you allegedly killed these people?

Chase: Yes.

Sheridan: You know you could be punished for it?

Chase: Yes, I know that.

Sheridan: Because these people here have other duties to perform other than sit here and listen to some fabricated story. We must investigate further the truth of your alleged confession of these three deaths and are about ready to quit here this morning at 3:15 A.M. Is there anything else you want to tell us?

Chase: No, I guess there isn't anything else I can think of. I thought of something else. This comes under Federal. My mother was getting allotment checks for my brother, government allotment checks, and I took these out of the mail and broke them open, signed Mother's and dad's names and then cashed them.

Sheridan: How many did you cash?

Chase: Five.

Walsh: Where did you cash them?

Chase: Out at Ole's.

Warnock: How long ago?

Chase: A year ago before Christmas.

Sheridan: Were they five separate monthly checks?

Chase: Yes.

Sheridan: Over a period of five months?

Chase: Yes.

Sheridan: One each month?

Chase: Yes.

Walsh: What year was this?

Chase: 1950.

Warnock: Around Christmas time?

Chase: Yes.

Warnock: Five months before Christmas?

Chase: About 2 or 3 months before Christmas.

Warnock: It started and ran through Christmas into 1951?

Chase: Yes.

Sheridan: Were they made payable to your mother and father jointly?

Chase: No, just my mother.

Warnock: Did you attempt to change the handwriting in conformity to copy your mother's and dad's?

Chase: I wrote my mother's signature the way she would and my dad's the way he would.

Warnock: Did your mother say anything?

Chase: They called me back on it.

Sheridan: The Treasury Department made no investigation?

Chase: No.

Sheridan: In other words your folks made no complaint to the government authorities?

Chase: No.

Walsh: Did you ever hit or try to choke or kill anybody in the army?

Chase: I got two of them to my credit fighting in Baltimore—two negroes—that was a race riot.

Sheridan: Briefly, did you set that fire at Camp Meade?

Chase: No.

Sheridan: Did anyone die as the result of fires you set while in the Army?

Chase: Not that I know of.

Sheridan: Was there one property damage suit?

Chase: There was one at Fort Meade, almost a million dollars.

Walsh: Can you remember the circumstances under which these fellows died? What part did you play in it?

Chase: A fight started up. We was fighting there.

Sheridan: Did you choke them to death?

Chase: Used chairs and everything else.

Walsh: You said you had two to your credit?

Chase: I think I do. I really don't know. There was six of them killed. We was fighting with knives, bottles, anything we could get.

CHAPTER 16

Harold Glenn Chase was born April 15, 1929. His family was respected and lived in the Pinehurst region of Snohomish County, Washington, now the Beverly Park neighborhood in the southern part of the city of Everett. His thirty-three-year-old father, Arthur B. Chase, worked as a welder across in an automobile garage the street from their home. His thirty-one-year-old mother, Emma, was a homemaker. They owned their home, valued in 1930 at $2,500. The house presently on the site was built in 1978, so Chase's childhood home does not exist. The property is currently located only feet from the freeway, US Interstate 5.

Harold Chase was the youngest of four children. He had a stepsister who was sixteen years his senior, a sister who was six years older, and a brother who was two years older. Later in life, Chase described his family's financial situation as "very poor" during his childhood and "only fair" during his youth. He attended Roosevelt Grade School in Pinehurst from 1935 to 1943, completing the seventh grade. He then attended South Junior High School in Everett, Washington, from 1944 to 1945, completing the eighth grade. He had poor scholastic and attendance records.

The children's father did not allow them to bring friends into their home. He apparently objected to social life of any nature. Relations between Harold's parents were less than congenial, Chase later described them as bickering about one thing or another all the time.

"We had a happy childhood as far as I can remember. A few accidents as kids. I blame my sister for one accident that happened in Portland. She threw me down the steps and broke my collarbone. Said she slipped and dropped me. I was a small kid but I remember very plainly."

Harold's father described him as "big for his age" in a newspaper interview after he was later arrested for murder. He said Harold was "handy with his hands, a good sheet-metal worker, and a good worker." Above all, he loved horses. "One thing I would always rather do than anything else was to ride horses," Harold would recall in an interview while jailed and awaiting trial for murder. He was a great reader of detective stories and considered himself later in life to be a student of criminology.

Chase's father said his son was kind to animals and children. The youth showed little interest in girls, according to his father, other than as just friends. He would later state, "I don't understand how a boy as kind to kids and animals as he was could do the things he said he did," his father noted in a newspaper interview.

Later in life, Chase would relate, "I quit school after the ninth grade to go to work in the shipyard. I thought I knew more than the teachers. It was a mistake." In all documents and records, Chase's address is recorded as that of his childhood home. It appears that when he was in the area and not incarcerated, he lived with his parents.

After one year of intermittent work for the Everett Shipbuilding Company as a sheet-metal worker, Chase joined the US Army at the age of seventeen. "I never was in any trouble before the army. Not a bit." His father concurred, "I don't understand what could have happened to the boy. He was never in any trouble until he got out of the army. He was always a good boy before then." Chase claimed that his troubles began when he was struck in the head with a crowbar while in the service.

CHAPTER 17

On April 22, 1946, one week after his seventeenth birthday, Harold Chase voluntarily enlisted in the US Army for three years in Seattle, Washington. Because of his age, his mother cosigned the enlistment papers. After induction at Fort Lewis, Washington, and eight weeks of basic training, he was assigned to the Ordnance at Fort George G. Meade, Baltimore, Maryland. Before going to Fort Meade, he was sent to Aberdeen Proving Ground in Maryland for Ordnance School, starting July 13, 1946.

Aberdeen Proving Ground is the oldest active US Army proving ground. It opened on the shores of Chesapeake Bay in 1917, shortly after the United States entered World War I. There was a need for increased capacity to test the new, larger weapons being developed for US forces. Its location, near industrial centers and shipping hubs, provided an advantage over the facility it replaced, the Sandy Hook Proving Ground in Sandy Hook, New Jersey. It remains a very active facility today, with over 20,000 military, civilian, and contractor employees.

During Chase's time there, he was hospitalized at Station Hospital, Aberdeen Proving Ground, on September 25, 1946. After two days, he was transferred to Fort Meade General Hospital, where he stayed until he was discharged two months later on November 30, 1946. Later in life, Chase described being struck in the back of the head with a crowbar while he was on guard duty at Aberdeen Proving Ground. This was the traumatic head injury to which Chase would later attribute the change in his behavior.

Chase returned to duty December 1, 1946, and worked for two weeks until he left Fort Meade on a three-day pass December 14, to be followed by a thirteen-day furlough through December 29. During his accrued time off, he traveled by train to Everett, Washington, to visit his family. On his return trip, he changed trains in Chicago, headed for Baltimore. He was riding on the Pennsylvania Railroad train, The Golden Triangle, and departed Chicago at approximately 11:15 p.m. on December 28, 1946. About two hours into the trip, he got up to use the men's room. The train was traveling at an estimated thirty to forty miles per hour. As he was entering the washroom, the train started to brake. Chase reported being thrown against the wall and then grabbing a handle above the toilet to keep from falling to the floor, resulting in a sharp pain in his right wrist. He was concerned about a fracture and sought out a brakeman who wrapped his wrist in ice but refused Chase's request to stop the train at an unscheduled location so that he could have his wrist evaluated. A second brakeman gave him the same answer.

When the train reached Harrisburg, Pennsylvania, Chase got off and walked to a civilian hospital near the station, where his wrist was splinted and he was provided a supply of analgesic pills. He caught a later train to Baltimore and reached Fort Meade at 8:30 p.m., December 29, 1946. He went straight to the Fort Meade General Hospital and was admitted to the Reconditioning Section. Wrist X-rays showed no evidence of fracture and that his injury was only a sprain. He was apparently discharged from the hospital thirty days later on January 28, 1947. Subsequent investigation into the injury concluded the diagnosis was "sprain, wrist, right, mild." Chase filed a claim against the railroad for his injury.

Chase finally returned to active duty with the Nineteenth Ordnance MM Company at Fort Meade On January 29, 1947. Within eight weeks, fires began to occur on the base. On March 29, 1947 at 10:40 p.m., Fire Captain Hinkle responded to an alarm that the bandstand was on fire. The fire was rapidly extinguished and attributed to a careless smoker. On April 10, 1947, a caller reported that a wrestling mat in a basement storage closet was on fire. Records indicate that PFC Harold Chase was injured fighting the fire. It was observed that there was no electrical wiring in the closet.

On April 27, 1947, at 10:27 p.m., "H. Chase, firefighter," received a report that the bandstand was again on fire, this time after burning newspaper was placed underneath it. It required thirty-five minutes to extinguish the fire. At 10:55 p.m. that night, a grass fire was reported. A bundle of burning newspapers was discovered at the center of the fire, according to army notes contained in Snohomish county records.

On May 5, 1947, at 2:25 a.m., an alarm was received that an Ordnance School building was on fire. The building's fire sprinkler system was under repair. The blaze took over five hours to extinguish. It caused $10,000 damage to the building and destroyed contents valued at $61,500. Chase was noted to be at the scene, working harder than anyone else did.

After four months of duty, Chase left on a twenty-one-day furlough on June 9, 1947. The fires stopped. He traveled again by train to visit his family in Washington State. Returning to Fort Meade, he changed trains in Chicago, headed for Baltimore. The train left Chicago at 11:45 p.m. on June 27. While walking about the train at 3:00 a.m., Chase tripped on a wooden pencil and fell, resulting in left ankle pain. In Pittsburgh, two railroad doctors examined him and recommended that he go to a hospital. He was admitted to the Marine Hospital in Pittsburgh June 28 to July 7. Radiographs of the joint were negative for fracture or dislocation. He was treated "strapping, procaine injections, and other local measures, and improved, but still had ankle pain and required the use of a cane at discharge after a ten-day hospitalization. He was admitted to Fort Meade General Hospital for another month of therapy and eventually discharged on August 4, 1947. Subsequent investigation yielded a final diagnosis of "ankle sprain, left, severe." Chase again filed a claim against the railroad for his injury.

Chase returned to active duty on August 5, working thirteen days before being hospitalized again at Fort Meade General Hospital, this time for a broken arm. On August 23, 1947, the first of three hospital fires in five days occurred. Notably, Chase had been admitted five days earlier and apparently was still hospitalized. The first fire occurred in Building No. 1245, Station Hospital. Patients discovered it at 2:48 p.m. when they smelled an acrid odor. The fire was confined to a closet, which had previously contained no combustible material, to the right rear of the stage. Patients were questioned, but no one had been to the rear of the stage that day. Just after midnight on August 27, 1947, a fire developed in Ward S-2 Building 1266, Station Hospital. The fire itself was in the main hospital ward. On the right side of the ward, the floor under and wall adjacent to bed 1 were badly burned, as was the bed mattress. It was determined that someone had poured a combustible liquid under the bed and ignited it. An identical event had occurred directly across the aisle under bed 31. No evidence was found at either site, and it was felt by army investigators that "persons or parties are responsible for these fires." No additional hospital fires occurred after Chase was discharged on September 5.

A fire on the base in September resulted in tragedy. A one-story company storeroom was reported ablaze at 11:57 p.m. on September 16, 1947. The flames were extinguished in one hour and eighteen minutes, but not before company orderly George J. Bohotch, who slept in the building, was killed. Subsequent investigation revealed that the fire started in the southwest corner of the building, probably in a waste-paper container. Court records note that the "Fire occurred while Chase was stationed there and he was suspected." Available US Army records indicate that Chase was once again hospitalized at Fort Meade General Hospital from September 13 to 22. The reason for the hospitalization is not discernible from available military records, but may have been one of two episodes of ear infection that he suffered while in the US Army. Harold Chase was eighteen years old.

The following are excerpts from an undated memorandum from the Snohomish County prosecutor's archives.

(Fort) Fire Chief Charles Eckman and U.S. Army Criminal Investigations Detachment (C.I.D.) Agent Kenneth N. Denaker, Investigation Section, Fort George Meade, both suspected Harold Chase of setting fires that occurred at Fort George Meade while he was stationed there. That they tried to keep Chase under surveillance and at such time that he was being watched, Chase did not make any fires. A few weeks before Chase was transferred from Fort George Meade it was arranged for a soldier to sleep in the next bunk to Chase and observe his activities as much as possible but that did not develop any additional evidence against Chase of setting any more additional fires. It was believed at the time that Chase may have been wise that he was being watched and he did not do anything that would cause the authorities to apprehend Chase...

At the time of the Ordnance School fire, Harold Chase was at the scene of the fire and, in fact, he worked with the fire department and other men in an endeavor to put the fire out and it was noticed that Chase worked harder than any man on the scene...

Harold Chase was known to many soldiers and officers as "Firebug Chase."

The reason that Chase was suspected at the very beginning was that every fire that occurred at the Camp, he would be the soldier that would turn in the alarm and besides, he would help put the fires out...

Investigator Denaker and Fire Chief Eckman said that Chase was a "Lone Wolf" at the Camp, he had no friends that he associated with, and even men in his own company had very little to do with him...

On September 17, 1947, there was a very serious fire that occurred in the Company's supply building. The fire seemed to have originated in the orderly room and Sergeant George Joseph Bohotch was asleep in the orderly room at the time of the fire and by the time the fire department arrived to put the fire out the entire orderly room and other parts of the building were enveloped in flames and after the fire was extinguished, the fire chief and the military police found the body of Sgt. George Joseph Bohotch badly burned. After a medical examination it showed that Bohotch had died from the inhalation of smoke. The fire took place in the south portion of the building that is known as Building T-852. It was also used as the orderly room and troop commander office, F Troop, 3rd Cavalry...

The records also show that Harold Chase was admitted to the Fort George Meade hospital with a broken arm on July 9, 1947. After his arm was put in a cast a couple of days later he was sent back to his company, was re-admitted on August 18, 1947 and then on September 24, Harold Chase was transferred out of Fort George Meade...

In connection with the death of Sgt. Bohotch at the time it occurred Chase was still stationed at Fort George Meade and he was suspected at the time of setting the fire but no information or evidence of any value was obtained...

Harold Chase was also suspected in the three separate hospital fires at Fort George Meade but they were unable to pin anything on him regarding any of the fires that occurred at Fort George Meade.

On September 24, 1947, Chase was transferred out of Fort Meade to the 881st Ordnance Company, Camp Campbell, Kentucky. Five days later, he was transferred to the Detachment of Patients, Station Hospital, Camp Campbell. From there, he was transferred on October 3, 1947, to Percy Jones Hospital in Battle Creek, Michigan, where he remained a patient until his honorable discharge from the military on January 30, 1948.

The hospital, originally built as the Battle Creek Sanitarium, had fallen into receivership and closed in 1933, during the Depression. The US Army purchased the buildings in 1942 and established the Percy Jones General Hospital. The hospital specialized in neurosurgery, plastic surgery, and the fitting of artificial limbs, treating approximately 100,000 military patients before it closed permanently in 1953. From an outsider's viewpoint, it would appear that the army was using Chase's hospitalization there to prevent him from committing further acts of arson. Chase was discharged after serving twenty of the thirty-six months for which he had volunteered. Of the 601 days Chase spent in the army, 303 (50 percent) were on active duty, 259 (43 percent) were as a hospital inpatient, and 39 (6 percent) were spent on leave.

During his twenty-month military career, Chase is suspected to have committed at least nine acts of arson, one involving a death. The fires caused approximately $100,000 dollars in damage at the time, which equates to over $1 million damages in 2013 dollars. This is in addition to the two people he claimed to have killed in a Baltimore race riot while stationed there, but for which documentation has not been located.

I publically requested Chase's army records from the National Personnel Records Center (NPRC) by standard protocol. It is somewhat ironic that a fire occurred at the NPRC in 1973, destroying or damaging sixteen to eighteen million official military personnel files. The military branches and years affected included air force discharges from 1947 to 1964 (75 percent of the records were lost) and army discharges from 1912 to 1960 (80 percent of the records were lost). Some documents for individuals whose records were destroyed in the fire were subsequently located elsewhere, sent to NPRC, and assembled into partial records. That is largely the case with Chase, although several of the photocopies received showed burned edges on the pages. The cause of the fire was never determined.

CHAPTER 18

Leaving behind a swath of death and destruction despite the brevity of his army career, Chase moved back home with his parents in Pinehurst, Washington. In the course of four weeks, Chase set at least five fires before he was arrested for arson. He provided the following statement to authorities:

March 29, 1948

Statement of Harold G. Chase discussing fires set in his neighborhood following his return from the US Army. Transcript from the Snohomish County Court records.

My name is Harold Glen (sic) Chase. I am nearly 19 years old and live with my parents Mr. and Mrs. Art Chase...in Pinehurst. I am voluntarily making this statement for the purpose of clearing up the fires I set in Pinehurst.

On Sunday, February 29, 1948, my mother and I were driving through Pinehurst when we saw firemen fighting a fire at the tabernacle. I joined in the fighting and was complimented on my work. That night I had trouble sleeping on account of smoke in my lungs. Then I went to the latrine in the basement, after slipping on some clothes. Then I went over to Foster Lowell's house and entered his basement. I wanted to see if I was really as good a firefighter as people said I was, so I set fire to some old window shades, etc. in the basement. After it got burning, I left the basement, hooked the door and went home. Then I went home to my room and waited. This was probably between 1 and 2 A.M. However, nothing apparently happened although I heard Mrs. Lowell call out. I wondered why the fire had not burned. A few nights later, on a Thursday, about 9:30 or 10 P.M. I started to walk to the home of Lyle Jones. Instead, I again entered the Lowell basement and piled some stuff at the same location, set it on fire and then went home and listened to the radio with my parents. When I heard people yelling, I went outside and then went to Lowell's and helped put out the fire. Toward the end the smoke was so thick I had to use an old gas mask that I borrowed from a neighbor. Before setting these two fires, I thought that no one was at home.

I think that it was the next Saturday, or possibly the Saturday after, I went to visit a girl friend. Afterwards I went home, did a little writing and started to go to bed about 3 or 4 A.M. I got to thinking then about setting fire to Ben McLean's woodshed. Finally I went over and into the shed and piled some chips and wood together and set them on fire. As soon as the fire got started good, I went back to my room and waited. About fifteen minutes later, I saw the glare of fire. Looking out, I could see the flames were pretty high and I was afraid it might jump over to Welk's garage. Then I got dressed and ran over and helped extinguish the fire.

I think it was Monday, March 15, that I attended a fireman's meeting near Seattle and I got home about midnight or later. Before going to bed, I walked to the rear of the house to make sure the back door was locked. Then I noticed the door to the old garage of ours was unlocked. I then went into the garage and set fire to some old inner tubes that were on the back seat of the old Dodge sedan. Then I went to my room. Occasionally I looked out toward the garage, but there was no sign of fire, so I went to sleep. My mother woke me up later, calling fire. I ran out to help fight the fire. I got between the car and the wall of the garage and took the hose line Mr. Thoren passed through a hole. My dad was using the Pyrene. We finally got the fire out. During this time I got gassed up and had to go to the hospital for the rest of the night.

Last Friday night, Mar. 26th, at about 10:15 I went out to our old feed house. It was pretty dull, so I emptied some rags from a carton onto the floor, placed the carton on top and set it on fire. Then I phoned Fire Chief Brown and told him it was not very bad but to come and take a look at it. Then I saw that the wind was causing it to start to blaze, so I notified Welk and stretched our hose over. Chief Brown arrived then and instructed me to put the fire out.

I have carefully read the foregoing statement in its entirety and same is a true and correct account of the facts in this case. I have not been threatened or abused and have not been made any promise of immunity. Having been advised that everything herein may be used against me, I am signing this voluntarily.

Signed—Harold G. Chase

CHAPTER 19

Chase spent most of the rest of 1948 in jail. He was arrested March 30 for the crimes he admitted committing and incarcerated through May 21, while his arson activities were investigated. Chase was evaluated by a psychiatrist in jail. During that time, he also was sent to Seattle for an independent psychiatric evaluation. He saw Dr. Ralph M. Stolzheise, a physician specializing in neuropsychiatry and child guidance. One day after Chase's nineteenth birthday, a summary letter was written to the Snohomish County Superior Court. In it, the psychiatrist made a number of observations and conclusions. He noted that Chase's history suggested or demonstrated personality traits including "emotional immaturity," "strong desire for recognition," "feeling of inferiority," and "preoccupation with pornographic writing and daydreaming."

With regard to Chase's obsession with arson, the physician observed, "The history of setting fires as a child; the history of having been involved in fire fighting and suspected of setting fires in the Service; and the present series of fires with which he is charged suggests a fetish mechanism."

The final paragraph of the report is quite perceptive and predictive of the future.

NEIL BRADLEY HAMPSON, MD

It is my opinion that we are dealing with a boy who is able to tell the difference between right and wrong, but who is activated by irresistible impulses. Such a personality is characterized by the diagnostic terms, psychoneurosis with pathological emotionality and obsessive-compulsive phenomena of the fetish type. It is possible that such a sick individual can be recovered with long sustained psychotherapy and custodial care. Penal handling of such a problem is of no value but under no circumstances should this individual be free on his own responsibility until therapy has brought about recovery.

(An unknown person added the underlining by hand on the court-filed report.)

The documents available from this period of Chase's life state that his impulses were irresistible, and he should not have been free in society until long-term institutionalized treatment resulted in recovery. After release from jail on May 31 pending trial, Chase was subsequently rearrested as cases were developed against him for each of the fires he had set. He was arrested July 16 and charged with first-degree arson, and then released on a $3,000 bail bond. He was rearrested November 2 for first-degree arson, and then released on another $3,000 bail bond. He was finally arrested December 11, charged with second-degree arson, and remained in jail until trial.

CHAPTER 20

On December 22, 1948, Harold Glenn Chase was brought before Superior Court of the State of Washington to answer to the charge of arson in the second degree for the burning of his neighbor's home. He pleaded guilty. He returned to court the following day for sentencing. His counsel, however, requested a ninety-day postponement of sentencing. During that time, Chase's attorney proposed that Chase be voluntarily admitted to Northern State Hospital in the town of Sedro-Woolley for psychiatric evaluation to determine his most appropriate placement. The court agreed.

A few days later, Chase's father, Arthur, accompanied his defense attorney to a meeting with Dr. E. A. Posell, medical director of Northern State. They discussed Harold's situation. On December 28, 1948, Dr. Posell wrote to the court, "This boy is properly in need of observation and treatment for a mental condition." He proposed a voluntary admission for ninety days, with a decision regarding long-term commitment or short-term extension after that time, depending upon the findings.

In the first decade of the twentieth century, the State of Washington had two hospitals for the criminally insane and needed another. The town of Sedro-Woolley in the northwestern part of the state wanted to diversify its economy. Legislators for the area put forth strong bids for the institution's location in Sedro-Woolley, and the site was selected. The doors to the asylum opened to patients in December 1912. From the beginning, locals referred to the institution as the "Bughouse." Bughouse was, in fact, an accepted synonym for "insane asylum" in the 1913 edition of *Webster's Dictionary*.

Northern State Hospital was known for its humane treatment of residents, as compared to other asylums for the insane. Most of those living at Northern State were there under commitment for long-term care. Those who worked at the hospital before it closed in 1973 are said to have commented later that many of those committed could easily have lived outside in modern society. One particularly bothersome example is that some husbands had their wives committed when they became "hysterical," presumably experiencing the normal effects of menopause. By the 1940s, many advances had been made, coincident with improvements in psychiatric care nationwide.

Chase arrived at Northern State at about the time that the popularity of a famous and controversial surgery called transorbital lobotomy peaked. The surgery was performed worldwide for a variety of psychiatric illnesses. In this procedure, a probe was introduced above the eye and passed to the back of the orbit. The instrument was struck with a mallet to drive it through the thin bone wall into the brain. It was then rotated in an attempt to destroy the prefrontal cortex area of the brain and control the malady from which the patient suffered. Northern State received great attention when it was rumored to have performed a transorbital lobotomy upon a then-famous patient, actress Frances Farmer. However, the rumor was just that, and the actress did not undergo the surgery.

Harold G. Chase was voluntarily admitted to Northern State Hospital on January 5, 1949. His inpatient psychiatric records are sealed, but he apparently did well there, outside of the murder he later admitted committing. As previously documented, the hospital medical staff judged the strangulation death of patient Leonard Lewis to be a suicide. In a letter to the court on March 22, 1949, shortly before the end of Chase's ninety-day observation period ended, his attending physician, Dr. P. R. Newkirk, wrote, "Since admission, Harold has cooperated very well with the hospital routine. He is helping the nurses and the orderlies with the care of the patients on the receiving ward. He is not psychotic but might well be diagnosed as 'psychopathic personality (arsonist type).' He has received psychotherapy and we believe that this has not been without influence on his psychology. In cases like Harold Chase's, psychotherapy should be continued for at least one year, possibly more, and the patient should be held to keep, without fail, in contact with his psychiatrist. Chase is willing to continue the treatments he is receiving here at present. If Chase has to serve a sentence, psychotherapy should be re-initiated at least 6 months before parole. In case the Court should decide upon a suspended sentence, Chase should be ordered to remain under psychiatric care for a considerable period of time at the pleasure of the Court. If this is done, we are confident that Chase will not commit acts of incendiarism. Such a prediction can, of course, be made only within the restriction that human behaviors cannot be predicted with absolute certainly under any conditions. We feel, however, that this plan would promise better results than incarceration of the delinquent."

Just prior to Chase's April 4 discharge, Dr. Newkirk wrote another letter to the court, saying, "Harold Chase was presented to the Staff today and consensus was that the diagnosis should be changed from Without Psychosis, Psychopathic Personality, Arsonist to Without Psychosis, Psychoneurosis, Pychasthenic Type."

CHAPTER 21

D r. Newkirk's words, in addition to Chase's history of suspected arson while he was in the military and the private psychiatrist's recommendation that "under no circumstances should this individual be free on his own responsibility until therapy has brought about recovery" guided the court's decision on April 8, 1949, when Chase returned for sentencing. He was ordered to "be confined in the Washington State Reformatory at Monroe, Washington, for the maximum term provided by law, to wit: ten years, with a recommended minimum of three years, in light of facts presently made known to the Court."

In the next paragraph of the court order, however, execution of the sentence was suspended for a period of three years, contingent upon Chase getting ongoing care from Dr. Newkirk of Sedro-Woolley, performing routine parole procedures, and remaining within the State of Washington. The court further ordered that "upon the fulfillment of the conditions of this probation by said defendant for the entire period thereof, the defendant may, upon proper application therefore at any time prior to the expiration of the maximum period of punishment for the offense of which he has been convicted, be permitted to withdraw his plea of guilty and enter a plea of not guilty and the Court shall thereupon dismiss the Information against the said defendant and said defendant shall thereupon and thereafter be released from all penalties and disabilities resulting from the offense of which he has been convicted."

Chase was freed on parole in April 1949. According to records, he returned several times for outpatient consultation with Dr. Newkirk.

CHAPTER 22

Following Chase's release, Sheriff Tom Warnock decided to take Chase under his wing and try to rehabilitate the young man. He appointed Chase to the new Snohomish County Sheriff's Posse. Historical photographs in which Chase appears in uniform; transcribed interviews with other deputies, in which they discuss working with him; and a 1953 letter from State of Washington Insurance Commissioner William A. Sullivan and Assistant State Fire Marshal E. L. Smith to John R. Cramer, warden of Washington State Penitentiary at Walla Walla, document that appointment. Chris Gee of Snohomish, Washington, who is currently a member of the posse and has been for a long time, said he was under the impression that a candidate had to be twenty-one years of age to join in 1949 because the posse was affiliated with the Snohomish County sheriff's office and the sheriff deputized all its members to special deputy status. Chase turned twenty that year, so an exception was apparently made.

Mike Radovich of Lake Stevens, Washington, current posse captain, states that when the posse was founded in 1949 at the South Everett Fairgrounds, each member was required to work as a deputy eight hours per month to maintain his commission, in addition to providing four hours of county jail service. The main function of the posse was to represent the sheriff's office in parades and at other public celebrations, participate in competition riding, and perform public service.

As Chase was six-foot-one and weighed from 220 to 240 pounds, it is possible that he lied about his age. Various documents created during his life list his year of birth as 1927, 1928, or 1929. (The latter is correct). Labels on posse photographs show that he went by "Glenn Chase," using his middle name as his first name. In any event, he appears to have been a member starting in 1949. "It was the happiest time of my life. A year and a half," Chase would later recall.

The following is an excerpt from Sullivan and Smith's 1953 letter.

Chase became a member of the Sheriff's posse and on occasion accompanied deputies during their routine work. During this period Chase went with officers and an agent of the F.B.I. to the small town of Silvana, following a bank robbery there. Officers detected tracks of the get-away car and followed same up a road. Shortly thereafter, Chase reported to the officers that he had found a one-dollar bill farther along the road. An examination of the bill revealed that it was bone-dry, whereas it was known that a heavy rain had occurred following the robbery. Under questioning Chase admitted that he had "planted" the dollar bill...

On another occasion, as Chase was driving his father's truck up the highway, he arrived at the scene of a wreck; on that occasion, a car had accidently left the road and run down a bank, trapping the driver. Chase watched the rescue operations for a while and then proceeded up the highway. As he later described it to the investigators, he had a sudden urge to drive his own truck down a bank and did so. Chase claimed that he also had been trapped under the truck, but Sheriff's deputies stated

that that there were clear shoe prints in the dirt, indicating that Chase
had pushed the truck down the bank.

In June 1949, Chase was apparently at the Fourth Annual Timber
Bowl celebration in Darrington in his role as a posse member. On Sunday
afternoon, a car containing six young people aged eighteen to thirty-three
drove off a nearby mountain road. The car dropped over a brushy, 150-
foot cliff, and plunged into the treacherous Saulk River. Initially missing
and presumed dead were Patricia Harbin, eighteen, and Raymond Ratcliff,
thirty-three, both of Darrington. The injured were Clem Ratcliff, thirty-
three; Gene Wilson, twenty-one; Helen Bannister, nineteen; and Helen
Lundquist, eighteen.

Witnesses said the car carrying the six young people was descending a
hill in a line of traffic on a road on which only one-way travel was permitted. Suddenly the car swung out of line, veered across the road, and hung
for a moment on the brink of the hill, held in place by a small sapling.
Then, before the eyes of horrified onlookers, the car broke loose, and shot
down the cliff and into the river.

According to Gene Wilson, the car landed on its roof in the water. He
said he attempted to dive for Patricia, but it was to no avail in the swift
current. At least four witnesses reported seeing Raymond Ratcliff thrown
from the car and swept downstream. At a riffle a thousand yards downstream from the accident, onlookers described seeing Ratcliff stagger to his
feet. But he was too weak to make his way to safety, fell back into the river,
and was swept on downstream.

According to current Darrington resident Bob Ensley, who was present at the time, a member of the posse rode his horse through town, saying that he was going to try to help rescue the accident victims. Chase

recounted later that he had been at the scene and dove into the river in a rescue attempt. His battle with the river current thrilled onlookers while he tried to reach the car. "They treated me like a hero that day," he recalled. When Chase met Ensley two years later at the Darrington movie theater, he recognized him as the posse member who had ridden his horse through town, lending credence to Chase's claim of making a valiant rescue attempt in the river.

Sullivan and Smith recounted the event slightly differently when they wrote, "Upon arrival, Chase dove into the river and barely escaped with his life. According to the deputies, there was no need for Chase's act, except to draw attention to himself."

It is also noted that Chase's January 1952 jailhouse confession included his burglary of the Casino Tavern in Everett in the summer of 1950 when he was still a special sheriff's deputy. He had been present at the close of business as part of his deputy duties and knew that the managers stored the money in the icebox.

CHAPTER 23

On December 11, 1950, Chase met Dr. R. R. Bradley in an Everett bar. According to County Prosecutor Phillip Sheridan's notes, Chase had been drilling with the sheriff's posse earlier in the evening and was wearing his uniform. After offering to give an inebriated Bradley a ride home, Chase instead drove to Smith Island, north of Everett, and strangled Bradley to steal the money he had seen him carrying in the bar. After killing Bradley and robbing him of $538, Chase drove his body to Everett General Hospital and called for help. He told attendants in the emergency ward that the man had apparently suffered a heart attack. A nurse checked Bradley's pulse and announced that he was dead. There was no doctor in attendance.

County Coroner Ken Baker, in relating events of the night of Bradley's death, said he, Clarence DeMars, and J. D. Lorraine, who were sheriff's deputies, were called to Everett General Hospital, where they found Bradley's body in the front of Chase's pickup truck. The body was taken to the county morgue. Baker said that there was no external evidence of foul play. Then, Baker, DeMars, Lorraine, and Chase went to the home of Bradley's wife to inform her of his death. Baker said Chase sympathized with her, saying that he wished he had some medical knowledge so that he could have helped Bradley.

Baker said that he told Mrs. Bradley that he could not order an autopsy because there was no evidence of foul play. He told her that she could have a private autopsy performed, but she declined. Baker had a limited budget, which severely restricted the number of autopsies he performed. In 1947, the county budgeted $200 per year for autopsies. By 1952, the amount had risen only to $1,000. Bradley's cause of death was formally recorded as "sudden death due to coronary thrombosis," without an autopsy. He was entombed in Everett's View Crest Abbey Mausoleum. Chase spent the $538 he stole from Bradley over a week's time in Seattle bars.

The investigation of Bradley's death included an interview with the sheriff's deputies who were on duty that night. The following is a transcript of one of them. In it, the deputy reaffirms Chase's role as a sheriff's deputy and describes Chase's suspicious demeanor.

January 17, 1952
Statement of J. D. Lorraine, Snohomish County Deputy Sheriff
Taken by Prosecuting Attorney Phillip Sheridan

Sheridan: Do you remember what happened on the evening of December 12, 1950?
Lorraine: Yes
Sheridan: Where were you that night, Mr. Lorraine?
Lorraine: I was in a sheriff patrol car with Clarence DeMars.
Sheridan: Do you know where you were?
Lorraine: In the Sheriff's Office.
Sheridan: Do you know who called?

Lorraine: No, I don't. I believe it was the nurse superintendant at General Hospital.

Sheridan: General Hospital?

Lorraine: That's right.

Sheridan: Do you know who was jailing that night?

Lorraine: Well, I can't tell you off hand.

Sheridan: What time of night was it?

Lorraine: Somewhere around 11:00 o'clock. A little after possibly.

Sheridan: Where did you go after you got the call?

Lorraine: We headed out to the hospital.

Sheridan: Did you know what you were going to the hospital for? Did DeMars tell you?

Lorraine: I was in the office when the call came in. They said Chase had a dead man in his truck, for us to get out to General Hospital right away.

Sheridan: But you didn't know the name of the dead man at that time?

Lorraine: I believe it was mentioned, Phil.

Sheridan: It's hard to recall something that happened thirteen months ago.

Lorraine: That case has kind of been on my mind all the time.

Sheridan: You knew you were going out to see Bradley who was alleged to have died?

Lorraine: That's right.

Sheridan: Did you see Chase out at the hospital?

Lorraine: That's right.

Sheridan: What part of the hospital was he in?

Lorraine: He was standing by the side of the truck when we drove in.

Sheridan: In the ambulance entrance?

Lorraine: That's right.

Sheridan: At the backend of the building?

Lorraine: That's right. They hadn't removed Dr. Bradley. He was still sitting propped up in the truck. He was sitting back in the corner. His head was thrown back, his mouth was partly open.

Sheridan: Was he wearing glasses then?

Lorraine: No. He didn't have glasses on.

Sheridan: Did the nurse say anything while you were there?

Lorraine: She was talking to (Coroner) Ken Baker most of the time and Chase came over and talked to us.

Sheridan: What did he tell you fellows?

Lorraine: He was pretty much excited. He was wondering what was going to happen to him he was in so much trouble and that was going to be bad.

Sheridan: He mentioned that he had been in trouble, that this would be bad?

Lorraine: Yes.

Sheridan: Did you ask him what happened?

Lorraine: I didn't. DeMars asked him what his story was. The story to DeMars was that he and the bartender, I believe he called him Sullivan, at the Monte Cristo, and Bradley had been in there drinking and Bradley partly slumped at the table or the bar and this bartender wanted to call a taxi and send Russ home. Chase insisted on taking him home. He said he knew him and had been drinking with him. He would put him in his pickup and take him home. Chase was very much agitated, couldn't stand still, and seemed to be laboring under quite a nervous strain. You know what I mean, couldn't talk coherently, that is, he would blubber when he talked. He started to tell us all about it. He made the statement that Dr. Bradley had vomited in his car.

Sheridan: Was there any evidence of any vomit?

Lorraine: No, there was no vomit in his car. Dr. Bradley did have his shirt front here wet.

Sheridan: Could you smell alcohol on Bradley? Was he drinking pretty heavy?

Lorraine: Yes. I knew him a long time. He worked on my eyes. It hadn't been two days since I paid him my last bill. I knew Dr. Bradley pretty well. Baker asked DeMars and I if we would help get the body out of the truck. We put the stretcher down, put the sack down, and put him in the sack. The nurse I believe asked DeMars what they were going to do about this. I think her name, if I am not mistaken, was Johnson. Anyway, she was the superintendent of nurses on that shift. He said, I don't know of anything except have him go down and make out a report. I believe DeMars made a remark about the doctor's face being blue. I don't see too good but I could notice Bradley's face was discolored.

Sheridan: Did I understand you to say he made that comment to the doctor? Lorraine: No, to Baker. There was no doctor there. We brought Russ in. Baker went through his belongings. We put him in the ice box.

Sheridan: Did you know anything about his clothes? Whether his pants had been opened?

Lorraine: No his trousers weren't opened but his pockets had been gone through.

Sheridan: How did you know that?

Lorraine: I know Dr. Bradley carried money. I had been on a couple of different drinking expeditions with him. There was only a small amount

121

of money in his pocket, probably not to exceed $2.00.There was no billfold.

Sheridan: No billfold?

Lorraine: I don't think so. Mr. Baker went through his belongings and put them in an envelope over at the morgue. He got Clarence and I as witnesses what had been taken out of his clothes (sic). I believe there was a check that hadn't been cashed.

Sheridan: How much was it for?

Lorraine: About $18 or $20. I believe there was a check and I think $1.30 in currency. His wristwatch was gone, his billfold was gone. I know he usually wore glasses but we saw no glasses at that time. I don't remember of having seen them.

Sheridan: You are sure there wasn't any wallet and glasses and there was some small currency?

Lorraine: I believe it was in his jacket pocket.

Sheridan: You mean in his vest pocket?

Lorraine: Yes.

Sheridan: His overcoat is missing.

Lorraine: There wasn't any out there.

Sheridan: His Shrine pin was missing?

Lorraine: That's right.

Sheridan: He didn't have a lapel pin on?

Lorraine: No he didn't.

Sheridan: You say Chase was very nervous?

Lorraine: Yes.

Sheridan: Did the nurse say anything about him bringing him up there?

Lorraine: She talked to DeMars about it. Chase stayed with me over by the car.

Sheridan: He did say, Why did all this happen to me, because I am in trouble, it will get me in more trouble?

Lorraine: Yes.

Sheridan: He seemed quite nervous.

Lorraine: Yes.

Sheridan: He complained about Bradley vomiting in the truck?

Lorraine: No, he didn't complain to us.

Sheridan: Well, what was the conversation?

Lorraine: He was just excited.

Sheridan: There was some talk about vomit?

Lorraine: Not that we could see. I helped lift Bradley out of the truck. Ken could give you more on that because I was on the wheel side of the truck. I pulled Bradley's feet out under the wheel to let him down.

Sheridan: You heard DeMars say his face looked blue?

Lorraine: There was a lot of discoloration for that short of time. When we pulled in, Ken hadn't got out of the ambulance. We drove in, Baker had just got there just ahead of us. In fact, we could hear his siren going.

Sheridan: Did Baker say anything about the discoloration?

Lorraine: No, not that I heard.

Sheridan: Did Chase hear DeMars' remarks?

Lorraine: I don't think he did.

Sheridan: Where was Chase after you got to the morgue?

Lorraine: He went to the office.

Sheridan: Did you folks later on go to Bradley's home?

Lorraine: Yes.

Sheridan: Was Chase with you?

Lorraine: Yes.

Sheridan: Do you know what he had to say out there?

Lorraine: No. I stayed in the car. DeMars and Chase went in.

Sheridan: Did Chase say anything on the way out?

Lorraine: No, he just sat in the back of the car.

Sheridan: Did he assist in removing Bradley from the pickup?

Lorraine: He did not.

Sheridan: He drove back up from the hospital to the Sheriff's Office?

Lorraine: Yes.

Sheridan: You left the morgue and went to the Sheriff's office before going to the Bradley home? Did he say anything at the Sheriff's office?

Lorraine: He went in and sat down and wrote out a report on it. I believe he sat in Buck's office and wrote out the report. It seems to me like Matlock was on. Whoever it was told him that report wasn't very satisfactory. He would have to do some changing in it. He was in the office for about a half hour. Then we took the car and went out to the Bradley home. Then we brought Chase down to his pickup and left. Chase didn't show much evidence of drinking, as much as he said he drank. He knew how to drive the truck.

Sheridan: Did you smell liquor on Chase?

Lorraine: I didn't get close enough to him because I don't like the fellow.

Sheridan: Why don't you like him?

Lorraine: I have my reasons.

Sheridan: Was he working as a deputy?

Lorraine: I don't think he was. He had a permit to carry a gun. Up at the fairgrounds we established the lost and found. Chase and I had quite an argument out there. That was pretty plain spoken. He never bothered me. I wouldn't go out with him in detail. I didn't want to get mixed up with him. In fact, in my estimation, he was gun happy. He had a badge and gun and thought he could throw his weight around.

Sheridan: Did you see him with a badge and gun?

Lorraine: Yes.

CHAPTER 24

In early 1951, Chase applied for a federal gun permit. As the telegram from Congressman Henry M. Jackson responding to Prosecutor Phillip Sheridan demonstrates, that permit was issued on February 13, 1951. Sheridan obviously wanted to know how this had happened. Jackson referred him to the Federal Building in Seattle for a copy of Chase's application. It is of historical interest that Jackson had served in Sheridan's position as Snohomish County prosecutor from 1938-1940.

From October 1950 through March 1951, Chase practiced mail fraud. He stole mail addressed to his mother containing monthly government checks, forged her signature, and cashed them. He was not caught.

His exact tenure as deputy is unknown, as the current Snohomish County Sheriff's Department does not maintain personnel records prior to 1980.

In mid-1951, it came to the attention of the Snohomish County Sheriff's Office through the Seattle Police Department that Chase was involved in the production of pornographic movies with Charles Edward Pauley of Seattle. These sources revealed that for several months, Chase had been spending his weekends in Seattle. He spent some of that time in a notorious First Avenue bar. On one of those occasions, Chase performed in a pornographic movie. He later complained to Detective Dick Wolph of the Seattle police morals detail that the others involved in the movie had blackmailed him.

In August, Snohomish County Deputy Sheriff John "Moose" Larson took Chase to see Detective R. F. Wolph. Chase led the officers to Pauley's apartment, and then insisted that Pauley show them some of the material. Pauley produced some obscene photographs and was placed under arrest. They searched his room and confiscated all obscene pictures and films. Chase admitted that he had performed, wearing a rubber mask, in one of the confiscated 16-mm films.

A charge of obscene pictures was filed against Pauley in King County Court. It was Chase's appearance at that hearing on September 4, 1951, that caused his delay in reporting for marshal work in Darrington until September 5. Pauley was found guilty of the charge. However, the matter did not end there. After Chase admitted under oath that he was one of the actors in the movie, Detective Wolph notified him that as soon as a woman witness was located, Chase probably would be charged with a morals offense, a felony. The woman was subsequently found and lodged in jail. However, Chase was not arrested because he fled to San Francisco.

In one of the numerous 1952 interviews following his confessions, a psychiatrist from Northern State Hospital asked Chase about the activity.

January 5, 1952
Everett, Washington
Interview with Harold Chase

Doctor: What about this hot picture stuff in Seattle?
Chase: That is a kinda embarrassing situation.
Doctor: Why?

Chase: For a fellow to get himself involved in anything like that.

Doctor: What is the so-called story of it?

Chase: I was going down to Seattle, down to Reno's bar there on 1st Avenue. I bumped into some fellows there and bumped into one fellow at the Liberty Theater. I would mention his name if I could. He introduced me to the photographer, and we started to go up to take pictures. I said if he would, we could get a little party up and go up to his apartment and see pictures, moving pictures. First thing you know someone mentioned------"oh no" I was interested as long as there was something to be interested in but I didn't think at the time that I was going to be the guinea. Nothing else was mentioned about it, and a month later we were down there and it was brought up again, and I had quite a bit of money in my pocket, from different deals that I had pulled, and I said OK let's make one. I was paid for the price, the price to them. I gave them all this money to get hold of the film. I got hold of a girl there and I figured all the time that Reno would be the one. He was sitting around drinking a lot. I never smoked a weed before and I think it was the weed. I got higher than a kite and was ready to go out and lick the world. The first thing I knew, I was talked into it and I was the guinea pig. My picture was made and there was nothing I could do about it then, except to try different ways to get a hold of it, and I finally got tired of it after about a year. It was eating on my mind and everything, what to do about it—I decided to do something about it—talked to one of the fellows down there at the sheriff's office there. I went into Sgt. Wolfe and made up a cock and bull story about being blackmailed and that was the reason I reported it. Finally we got hold of the film, and went up to the guy's apartment and waited for him and confiscated the film. The films are now at the police department in Seattle.

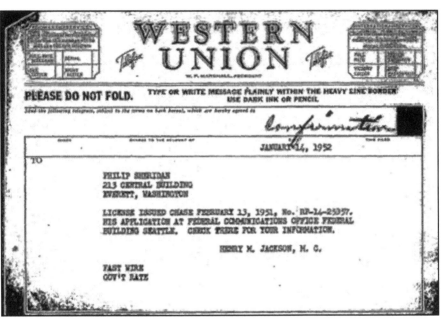

Telegram from Congressman Henry M. Jackson to Snohomish
County prosecutor, dated January 14, 1952, confirming that Harold
Chase had been issued a gun permit on February 13, 1951.

CHAPTER 25

As noted previously, Chase began as town marshal in Darrington on September 5, 1951, and then set the fire that consumed several downtown buildings on September 9, 1951. When Chase's confessions came forth in January 1952, there was public disagreement about how he came to be hired, since he was a convicted arsonist on parole. City Councilman Ed Hunter claimed that Chase was hired on the basis of a recommendation from the Snohomish County Sheriff's Office. He said Mayor A.B. Wheeler and Mel Garton, who was retiring as Darrington sheriff, visited the (Snohomish County) Sheriff's office and asked for a recommendation. Chase was recommended, Hunter said.

Sheriff Tom Warnock denied that anyone in his office had recommended Chase. "In fact," he said, "I didn't even know he was working up there."

Hunter disagreed. "It's a sad story. He was marshal four days before the fire. Chase was sent up here by the sheriff's department and recommended by them. We didn't know he had a past record. The sheriff's office sent him up here with a star on him, a deputy sheriff's commission, a Billy club hanging at his waist, and a big gun. We hired him, and four days later half the town burned down."

When Chase visited Darrington to talk about the marshal position, he was accompanied by his mother and another Snohomish County Deputy Sheriff. He was reportedly carrying a card commissioning him as a special deputy sheriff. The commission was seen by Mel Garton and a member of the volunteer fire department. Garton recalled, "Moose Larson brought Chase up here to see about the job and introduced him to me. I took Chase to see Mayor Wheeler."

While no town official had seen a letter of recommendation for Chase, members of the city council inferred endorsement from the fact that Deputy Larson accompanied him when he applied for the job. "Now we're having trouble pinning down just who in the sheriff's office recommended Chase. They're passing the buck among each other," said Hunter.

Later, in January 1952, Sheriff Warnock would say that said Chase's special deputy commission was canceled in mid-1950 when he was dropped by the Snohomish County Sheriff's Posse for failing to regularly attend practice. This contradicts Prosecutor Sheridan's notes that Chase was drilling with the posse earlier in the evening that he killed Bradley in December 1950 and wearing his special deputy uniform that night. It is not clear that the issue was ever resolved.

Despite Chase's unusual activity in the King Tut Theater the evening of the fire, when Chase confessed, he described stacking paper cartons against one side of the tavern and setting them afire. He then went to his room. After he could see flames leaping skyward, he drove the volunteer fire department's truck to the scene and began fighting the fire as described. The effort was futile.

Chase fled to San Francisco to avoid an interview about the fire under the effect of sodium pentothal, checking into the San Francisco YMCA on September 20, 1951. The subsequent investigation of his claim of murdering a tourist there involved an extensive examination of his contacts and activities in San Francisco.

Chase claimed to have met and killed "Joe" on October 10, 1951, the third Wednesday after his arrival. That night he and a friend named Frank went to the Skyroom in Chinatown and spent $150 "just eating and drinking and having a good time and getting drunk."

Investigators' reports revealed the following information about Chase's time in San Francisco, Chase became friendly with Jerry Cornell, who worked at a nearby Standard Oil gas station and let Chase park his car there in exchange for occasional use of the vehicle. Cornell recalled that on one occasion, Chase came back to the gas station with his clothes a mess. In his murder confession in 1952, Chase himself recalled that Cornell said, "What happened to you?" when he saw the orange soda on his coat. Lue Galloway, who worked at the Cleaning Shop, told investigators that Chase brought in a badly stained jacket on October 26 or thereabouts. She did not know the identity of the stain, but she was certain that it was not blood.

Another San Francisco acquaintance called Jarado borrowed Chase's car frequently. He cleaned it once and found pieces of broken glass, as well as a bloodlike stain on the ceiling above the passenger's seat.

Jarado said Chase was always thinking about women. He said Chase boasted about his sexual prowess and claimed that a kick to the testicles had rendered him sterile, and for that reason, "he was a good man for the girls to have." Chase and another resident frequented the Sky Room in Chinatown, where a Chinese woman named "Peg" showed him things he never knew of before. Chase told his friend that he was paying Peg quite a sum of money to have sex with him.

Chase dated a woman in San Francisco named Mildred Blackman once. They went for a drive, had dinner, and saw a movie. She told investigators that Chase was very talkative and wanted to tell her too much of his family history. She wasn't interested. Chase told her that he had been a police officer and that he was previously married. Kay Hill, a secretary at the YMCA, told investigators that Chase asked her for a date, but turned him down. She said Chase made her skin crawl.

Chase remained in San Francisco for approximately five weeks. Eventually, he was arrested on the outstanding Darrington warrant and returned to the Snohomish County jail on November 28, 1951. He made his amazing jailhouse confessions on January 5, 1952.

CHAPTER 26

Although Sheridan, the prosecutor, was not convinced that Chase had murdered Dr. Bradley, he sought an autopsy two years after the body was interred. Sheriff Warnock obtained permission from Bradley's widow, who had remarried, to exhume the corpse from View Crest Abbey Mausoleum for that purpose.

January 7, 1952
Statement of Mrs. Helen Bradley Hart, taken before Sheriff James Warnock

Warnock: To your recollection, what was the cause of his (Russell Bradley's) death?
Mrs. Hart: I was under the impression that it was a heart attack.
Warnock: How was his physical condition prior to this?
Mrs. Hart: It was very good.
Warnock: Can you quote his words regarding his condition?
Mrs. Hart: I can remember him saying something like, "I'm in perfect condition" but I don't remember his exact words.

Warnock: Well then, in regard to the money he apparently had...Do you think he did or didn't have money on his person?

Mrs. Hart: He was at the beach in the morning and unless he collected water money and I haven't found out that he did.

Warnock: If he did collect water money and was successful in his collections, what would be the amount due then?

Mrs. Hart: I don't know exactly but the units are $250 a unit but they wouldn't have had the cash. If they had checks he might have cashed them Monday morning.

Warnock: Then what day of the week was that?

Mrs. Hart: That he died?

Warnock: Yes.

Mrs. Hart: Monday night or before Tuesday morning.

Warnock: Can you just give me, from your recollection, the events that took place on that evening, when you were notified of his death?

Mrs. Hart: It must have been 1:30 at night and it was Mr. Baker, Mr. DeMarrs (sic), and Chase.

Warnock: And when did this take place?

Mrs. Hart: About 1:30 in the morning.

Warnock: What was the conversation between the parties concerned?

Mrs. Hart: Mr. Baker said "Mr. Bradley is gone," and Mr. Chase said that he told him the address but that he didn't understand him. He wanted to know if he had assistance. Chase said, "I wish I would have known something about medicine. I would have been able to save him."

Warnock: What transpired then, the next day?

Mrs. Hart: I don't remember if I went down to the coroner's office the next day. I looked for his shrine pin and his overcoat was missing. I don't know whether he left it someplace. However, there was money still in his wallet.

Warnock: How much money in his wallet?

Mrs. Hart: A little.

Warnock: In change or bills?

Mrs. Hart: I really don't know but Mr. Baker should have a report of it. Probably around $10.00.

Warnock: Well, when was it that you saw the body?

Mrs. Hart: That I saw the body?

Warnock: Yes.

Mrs. Hart: Down at Challacombe and Fickel Funeral Home and I think it was on Wednesday.

Warnock: Who did you see at the undertaking parlor?

Mrs. Hart: I think Mr. Challacombe and Walt Precht.

Warnock: What conversation took place?

Mrs. Hart: One of them said "He looked awfully funny." I said he didn't look natural. One of them said he certainly didn't look like himself. I felt that they all thought he looked like that.

Warnock: Could you get down to the points on this particular thing? It might be very helpful. What did they tell you?

Mrs. Hart: I just don't—

Warnock: Do you recall making any statements? I don't want to lead you in these questions.

Mrs. Hart: I thought that it might be from gas that he looked so funny. He looked all bloated up.

Warnock: Did you feel him anyplace? Where did you put your hand?

Mrs. Hart: I put my hand on his neck.

Warnock: In what location? Around his throat?

Mrs. Hart: Yes. He was very bloated and didn't look like himself.

Warnock: To your knowledge, his neck was swollen?

Mrs. Hart: Yes.

Warnock: Did the thought impress you at the time that in view of the fact that he had been in a good state of health, that it was peculiar that he would have a heart attack?

Mrs. Hart: Well, I thought it was strange that type of thing must have caused it because we went hunting two days before and brought home two deer. I shot one and was too weak to drag it very far so he had to drag it for me.

Warnock: That was a great deal of exertion wasn't it?

Mrs. Hart: Yes, it was.

Warnock: Did he show any after-effects after that?

Mrs. Hart: No.

Warnock: That must have proved he was in a pretty good state of physical health.

Mrs. Hart: He was as strong as he could be.

Warnock: How do you feel about your husband?

Mrs. Hart: I think it's logical that he might have met with foul play. It's possible, that part of it but I can't understand the money part of it. That sounds fictitious. It could have been. He wrote a check that night.

Warnock: Do you think that it is right, in view of the peculiar events that we have uncovered, that a post mortem be done?

Mrs. Hart: Yes. I think it should be done.

Warnock: Will you give your consent?

Mrs. Hart: Yes, I think we should find out the truth if we can.

Dr. R. B. Townsend signed Dr. Bradley's original death certificate, attributing the cause of death to heart disease. Since the discussion of exhumation and autopsy was ongoing, he sent the following letter to the county prosecutor, apparently to explain his cause-of-death diagnosis.

January 7, 1952

To Whom It May Concern;

During a social call which he made at my office a few weeks prior to his death, Dr. Russell R. Bradley mentioned that he had been doing a good deal of square-dancing and had noticed some shortness of breath after the exertion. He also stated that he planned to go deer-hunting and wondered if I should not examine his heart. I did so and found that while the heart sounds and blood pressure were normal, he was carrying a pulse rate of 120. On one or two previous occasions when I had examined him the same condition had existed. I therefore presumed that the heart had weakened and that this weakness was manifesting itself in shortness of breath. Accordingly, I told him that if he insisted in going hunting, he should at least not try to carry out a deer if he secured one. I did not see Dr. Bradley again before his death.

R. B. Townsend, M.D.

Tacoma pathologist Dr. Charles Larson and Everett physician Dr. Emmanuel Bitar performed Bradley's autopsy on the night of January 7, 1952. Sheridan, the prosecutor, announced, "The doctors are confident that Dr. Russell R. Bradley did not die of natural causes," but he withheld the actual findings of the autopsy "to avoid revealing my case to the defense." Based on the autopsy findings, Chase was arrested for first-degree murder on January 8, 1952. Sheridan cancelled Chase's appointment with a Northern State Hospital psychiatrist who planned to administer "truth serum" to Chase in an attempt to unravel further details of the Darrington story.

In an interview shortly following his arrest, Chase's mother said that the crimes he confessed were "only in his imagination." She related, "He never was cruel or vicious. I've seen him sit up all night with a sick animal. Glen (sic) has never been the same since he got home from Army service. They can get him to say anything they want him to say." Mrs. Chase noted that her son suffered a head injury while in Army training. "It changed his whole personality. You know, he really believes he did those things. But I know he didn't kill those men and he didn't start any of those fires, either." She also reported that Chase had written her from the army that he had suffered four arm fractures in accidents. Review of his army records documents only one broken arm.

Harold G. Chase, age twenty-two, at the time of his arrest for murder. Photograph by Ken Harris, *Seattle Post-Intelligencer* newspaper, January 10, 1952.

CHAPTER 27

As San Francisco authorities tried to get a line on a French tourist reported to have been killed while visiting in this country, the body of Leonard M. Lewis, the fifty-year-old mental patient who died in Chase's presence at Northern State Hospital in Sedro-Woolley, Washington, was ordered exhumed and autopsied. Lewis had been discovered strangled, with a towel tied around his neck. Hospital officials had ruled the death a suicide.

After the autopsy, Dr. Gale Wilson of Seattle reported that Lewis had died of strangulation as a result of a fractured larynx. He reported that he had "never seen such a fracture without a direct blow to the larynx." Skagit County Prosecutor Reuben Youngquist charged Chase with premeditated murder. The prosecutor asked for the death penalty. Chase entered a plea of innocent by reason of mental irresponsibility.

As part of the investigation, an interview with members of the Lewis family was conducted. The transcript follows.

Interview with Family of Leonard Lewis

Skagit County Sheriff: Will you start making your statement, Mr. Seemeyer (brother-in-law)?

Seemeyer: We went to Sedro Woolley down to the funeral parlor to see the body of Leonard M. Lewis.

Sheriff: Now just relate what happened at the home.

Seemeyer: We went into the funeral home and noticed bruises on the left side of his face. We noticed bruises on the left side of his throat and they even showed through the powdering of the corpse. Looked like evidence of quite a bit of brutality or evidence of a lot of beating or something.

Sheriff: Will you be more specific for the record here, in locating bruises on first the face and then the neck.

Seemeyer: Well, the one bruise started up around the temple and came down, as I can remember, more or less to the jaw.

Sheriff: Almost to the chin?

Seemeyer: Yes, and the other one almost to the throat.

Sheriff: Now, what was the condition of the throat? What did it look like just looking at first?

Seemeyer: Well...

Sheriff: With respect to its normal size.

Seemeyer: It was large. In fact, we thought if we wouldn't have known him personally, we wouldn't have recognized him at all. All the kids said that. He didn't look very natural because the throat was so swollen.

Sheriff: Do you remember calling this to the attention of someone in authority?

Seemeyer: No one in authority.

Sheriff: You had conversation with someone?

Seemeyer: Yes. Among the family.

Sheriff: Will you relate this.

NEIL BRADLEY HAMPSON, MD

Seemeyer: The conversation was between one of the sisters and one brother-in-law and my wife and myself. We first thought of an autopsy but this one sister-in-law was so shocked and upset that we forgot about it.

Sheriff: At the time, what was your opinion regarding his death?

Seemeyer: You mean, at the time of the...After I saw the body?

Sheriff: Yes.

Seemeyer: My very words were, "I think this guy was killed," and I still think so.

Sheriff: Now then, that's what—

Seemeyer: The next thing we were told was that my sister-in-law was told he was in restraints and they had a hand towel wrapped around his neck. It wasn't more than 22 or 24 inches long and that's what she was told.

Sheriff: What was the reason you contacted me?

Seemeyer: Well, we felt this way. That there is nothing we can do for him but if that is the treatment they get there, maybe we can help save somebody else up there.

Sheriff: You realize, don't you, Mr. Seemeyer, that sometimes there are circumstances that are not possible for the authorities to handle—the situations that develop that don't come to their attention.

If Chase's story was true, he would have killed Joe, the French tourist in San Francisco, in late September or early October 1951. But San Francisco authorities failed to find any evidence of a missing tourist or an unidentified body with injuries consistent with the mode of death that Chase described. US Immigration had no record of a missing French tourist. Following Chase's arrest and return to the Snohomish County jail, the red book in which he claimed to have written Joe's name was examined. Chase was unable to identify the entry in the book and said that he may have torn the leaf from the book. Snohomish County deputies searched the car in which Chase said he killed Joe and found shards of glass as well as stains on the seat. Snohomish County Sheriff Warnock decided not to pursue Chase's claim of murdering Joe because the San Francisco Police Department's extensive search had turned up no evidence of a crime.

A month after he verbally confessed, Chase reaffirmed his guilt in a handwritten letter to Sheriff Tom Warnock:

Everett, Washington
February 10, 1952

To Tom Warnock, Sheriff Snohomish County

I Harold G. Chase is writting (sic) this letter of my own free will. No one is making me do it.

Sometime in Dec. 1950 I met Dr. Bradley at the Monte Carlo Hotel. We sat and had some drinks. About 10 or 11 at night we went out to my car. We were going to Marysville, Washington. On the way I got the urge to kill him. He had about $538 on him. I went down the road going to the packing house. I get out of the car and went around to his side. I put my hands around his neck and killed him. I got the $538 from him and went to the hosp. in Everett, Washington. The rest is not so important.

Now that I have said it I'm happy it is done. I don't know what made me do it but I'm sorry I did it so help my (sic) God. This is the truth that I have written.

This statement is made up of two pages. I am freely and voluntarily signing.

Harold G. Chase

CHAPTER 28

Chase's trial for arson, scheduled to start on January 22, 1952, was postponed. On May 21, his trial for the January 28, 1949, murder of Northern State patient Leonard Lewis began in Skagit County Superior Court in Mount Vernon, Washington, before a jury of ten men and two women. On the first day of the trial, Snohomish County Sheriff Tom Warnock testified about the voluntary confession Chase made in the jailhouse on January 5. He described Chase's claim that he had strangled Lewis because "he got on my nerves," then arranged the body and scene to make it appear that Lewis had committed suicide. Hospital staff had agreed with that conclusion at the time, and Lewis's death had been considered a suicide until Chase confessed.

During the trial, the prosecutor said Chase had killed Lewis by knocking him out with a punch to the chin, and then strangling him. The undertaker who handled the funeral arrangements for Lewis testified that he noticed a bruise on the side of Lewis's face. Dr. Gale Wilson, the Seattle pathologist who performed the autopsy on Lewis's exhumed body, went into great detail about the implications of the fracture of the larynx. The fractured body part dissected from the corpse was introduced into evidence. He described the type of fracture as that caused by a sudden blow, such as one delivered by a fist or foot. Wilson stated that during World War II, many soldiers were taught a method of kicking a person who is lying down in order to fracture the larynges of enemies on the battlefield.

Under cross-examination, Wilson said it would be virtually impossible to self-inflict such an injury. He added that Lewis had sustained the fracture while he was alive, and that he could not have survived more than four or five minutes without medical attention.

Prosecutor Youngquist questioned witnesses closely concerning any threats, violence, or coercion that might have been used against Chase to "extract" the confession. E. O. Walker, a childhood friend who had known Chase since both were eight years old, stated he believed Chase's murder confessions because he had never known Chase to tell anything but the truth.

When the state rested its case, Chase's twenty-eight-year-old defense attorney, Paul Stocker, presented an opening argument that Lewis was severely depressed and had sought to kill himself. He said Chase's confession had been violently extracted from him, and that Chase enjoyed the publicity and celebrity that the confessions and subsequent actions had brought him. Stocker said that Lewis was attempting to commit suicide by refusing to eat and starving himself. Mrs. Ida Sheay, a registered nurse who was in charge of the Northern State ward when Lewis died, testified that the patient would not take nourishment and was being spoon-fed.

Stocker noted that Chase's confessions were taken after his attempted jailbreak from Snohomish County jail while he awaited trial on the charge of arson. He reported that Chase had been severely beaten, in fact to such an extent that he was "still passing blood two days later." Stocker called Chester Michaels of Snohomish to the stand. Michaels said that he was an inmate in the jail at the time of Chase's aborted jailbreak. He testified that he saw Deputy Sheriff Bob Lawe hit Chase once in the stomach and again in the face, the latter blow knocking the defendant out for a period of about fifteen minutes. Michaels stated that when Chase was shoved back into the tank in which they were being held, Chase was covered with blood about the face. He admitted under cross-examination that he saw no cuts on Chase and could not say what the source of the blood was.

Stocker said that when Chase made his first statement about having killed three people, he went from being a prisoner to being a celebrity. He claimed that Chase subsequently embellished his stories to enhance that celebrity. William Boswell, another defense witness, backed Stocker's observation. Boswell, a Snohomish County private investigator who was previously employed by the sheriff's department, testified that Chase was a person who sought attention and publicity. He told the jurors that after a story about Chase appeared in a detective story magazine, he took his copy to Chase to have him autograph it. Boswell said that at that time, Chase denied the truth of any of the incidents described in the magazine.

Dr. Johannes B. Thiersch, associate pathologist at the University of Washington, testified for the defense with regard to the fractured larynx. Handed the fractured larynx that had been removed from the exhumed body of Lewis, he testified that he could not give competent testimony as to whether the fracture was inflicted before or after death. He said that the advanced state of decomposition made it impossible to arrive at any conclusion, or to state whether the fracture was caused by manual strangulation or hanging. He said the larynx, which he had examined, was "suggestive but not convincing."

Under cross-examination, Dr. Thiersch agreed that the fracture could only have been caused by a "localized sudden trauma," but that it was possible for the larynx to have been broken by a pillow slip or something similar depending on a great many details, including how the body was positioned, whether there was a knot in the cloth, and whether the cloth had caught the victim under his larynx. Thiersch's testimony was intended to controvert Dr. Wilson's testimony that he had examined more than 200 larynges and had "never seen a fracture of this type result from hanging."

When Chase took the stand in his own defense later in the trial, he denied killing Lewis or anyone else, for that matter. Chase testified that he and two attendants at the hospital were playing cards when they heard "a whispering noise." They made a search immediately, and one of the attendants, Kenneth E. Goad, found Lewis in his room, dead.

Chase said Lewis was lying in a half-kneeling position on the bed, pitched forward. A noose made of a pillowcase and a hand towel was looped around his neck and fastened over the headboard of the bed.

Under cross-examination, Chase was asked why he had repeatedly claimed responsibility for Lewis's murder and now suddenly changed his story. Chase declared that his current claim of innocence was the truth. He said that he made the confession to divert the officers' attention from the attempted jailbreak on January 4, 1952, in which he had attacked the jailer. He admitted that after he started to tell the story of the murders, he "got carried away." He admitted that he enjoyed the publicity generated by the story.

The weeklong trial brought out considerable conflicting expert testimony as to Chase's mental condition, but all agreed that he was not insane from a medical standpoint. One witness, Dr. Edward A. Posell, said Chase had a personality disorder that prevented him from determining right from wrong. He added that Chase's basic instinct for self-preservation was not operating fully.

The twelve-member jury deliberated for nine hours before finding Chase not guilty. In his instructions to the jury prior to deliberations, the presiding judge suggested that the jurors might rule on both on his guilt or innocence on the second-degree murder charge, as well as his safety to be at large with respect to his present state of mental responsibility. The jury did not do so.

When Chase heard the verdict from jury foreman Roger Young, he commented, "Oh, boy." He then added, "I'm shaking like a leaf. I thought they were going to convict me!" Tears welled up in the eyes of Chase's father at the verdict, and defense attorney Paul Stocker performed a victory dance.

Immediately after the trial, Chase was returned to Skagit County Jail to await his transfer back to Everett and the Snohomish County Jail for his murder trial in the death of Dr. R. R. Bradley. Later, some would describe the prosecution's case against Chase in the Leonard Lewis murder as poorly prepared.

CHAPTER 29

On September 29, 1952, Chase went before Judge Charles R. Denney of Snohomish County Superior Court for arraignment on the charge of murder in the death of Dr. R. R. Bradley. Chase acknowledged his identity, said that he understood the charges against him, and entered a plea of guilty to second-degree murder. Plans for a trial were canceled.

The following day, Chase returned to court for sentencing. On September 30, 1952, he was sentenced to hard labor in the state penitentiary at Walla Walla for the remainder of his natural life. The previously suspended ten-year sentence for arson was to run concurrently. At the bottom of Chase's typed sentencing document, Judge Denney wrote by hand, "This defendant is dangerous. There is reason to think he may be psychopathic. This increases his menace to society."

In 2013, Chase's defense attorney Paul Stocker, age eighty-nine, shared with me a copyrighted manuscript that he had written about the Lewis trial. With his permission, I quote,

The following month, I negotiated a 2nd degree plea for Glenn in the Dr. Bradley case with Phil Sheridan, prosecutor in Snohomish County. The evidence in the Bradley case was conclusive. In my report to the Board

of Parolees, I joined with the Judge and the prosecutor in recommend-
ing a sentence of natural life for Glenn. I had protected the mother
from the most extreme pain of having a child executed but also had the
duty to protect society from a monster.

On Chase's Washington State Penitentiary commitment record, dated
October 3, 1952, he listed his religion as Protestant, occupation as welder,
and nearest friend as his mother.

Paul Stocker, Chase's defense attorney in his two murder
trials, at home in 2013 at age eighty-nine.

CHAPTER 30

As is required by Washington State law, within six months after the sentencing, the State of Washington Board of Prison Terms and Paroles met to review Chase's sentence of life in prison for the crime of second-degree murder. Despite recommendations by both the sentencing judge and prosecuting attorney that the minimum term be life confinement, the board on March 24, 1953, reduced Chase's term to fifty years. Further, "by good behavior and work record," he was allowed to earn an allowance of 16 years, 8 months off his sentence. Therefore, his minimum state of confinement would expire September 29, 2002. If he earned the maximum credit for good time served, he would be first eligible for consideration for parole on January 29, 1986.

Chase's prison records at Walla Walla Penitentiary are a matter of public record and were obtained through standard channels. Chase's Admission Summary, completed January 7, 1953, notes,

> Chase wishes to return to the home of his parents at Everett, Washington. He has an eighth grade education with a poor scholastic and attendance record. Tests conducted here indicate an IQ of 100,

or average; the MMPI (author's note: this is a standardized psychological inventory test) reveals a high psychopathic deviate and borderline hypomanic profile, indicating a lack of social understanding and an inability to profit from experience.

CHAPTER 31

A twenty-page letter dated September 22, 1953, from State of Washington Insurance Commissioner William A. Sullivan and Assistant State Fire Marshal E. L. Smith to Warden Cranor, mentioned earlier with regard to Chase's activities with the sheriff's posse, includes extensive information about Chase's arson activities in the army, in Pinehurst, and in Darrington, along with some mention of his other crimes. Little of the information was made public because Chase was never tried for arson. (He was sentenced for the Pinehurst fires but was not tried because he confessed.) The section of the letter relating to the investigation of the Darrington fire is reproduced here because it shows the scope of the investigation and the strong case it would have made against Chase if he had been tried.

Re: Harold Glen (sic) Chase, 23
        Fire: September 8, 1951 at 4:03 A.M.
        Darrington, Washington

    Properties involved were a motion-picture theater, owned and operated by Mr. & Mrs. Leonard Mabon Hamilton; a tavern, owned and operated by Mr. And Mrs. Thos. Furman Henson; and a shoe repair shop, owned and operated by Mr. Maurice F. Purcell. These one story frame buildings were attached, the longer tavern and motion-picture buildings being on either side of the shorter shoe-repair shop, thus formed a U-shaped building with the open end at the rear. This open end or court probably was about 12 feet wide and 20 feet deep.

It is important to mention that there was situated on the tavern side of this court, an 8-foot long fuel-oil tank, same having been mounted on above ground brackets. The tank was protected by a lean-to wood shingle roof and the ends of the enclosure were boarded solid, except for a wooden door (kept under lock). The front of the enclosure was boarded solid, except for a wooden door (kept under lock). The front of the enclosure was boarded solid to a height of about 4 feet or so and so the space from top of same to the underside of the lean-to roof was composed of open slats. So far as can be determined, the only openings were those between the slats.

The fire was discovered by one Harold Glen Chase, 23, the recently appointed night marshal. Chase sounded the fire siren, which called out the voluntary firemen and he also drove the fire truck out of the fire station.

Walter Bates, Fire Chief, was awake and saw the fire before the alarm. He started for the station and enroute saw night marshal Chase driving his car toward the fire station. When he arrived at the station, Chase had already started the siren and driven the fire apparatus outside. Fire Chief Bates then drove same to the scene of the fire, after instructing Chase to watch the stores and traffic.

A day or two before the fire, the wooden 4-inch water main, on the main street, about one-half block west of the fire, broke and flooded out over the surface of the street. This main was still out at the time the fire occurred. The pumper also had gear trouble during the fire. These two incidents contributed toward the firefighting difficulties and plus the start the fire got before firemen arrived, resulted in the loss of the three subject buildings. Minor damage was sustained by the adjacent building and those across the street. Later, an insurance adjuster said that the total loss would reach at least $40,000 with fire insurance coverage of only $19,000.

A couple days after the fire, information was received by town authorities, to the effect that their new town marshal, Chase, has a record as a 'fire setter'. After this information was received, the matter was reported to the Sheriff's Office and Under-sheriff "Buck" Weaver called Chase into the office and questioned him at length. However Chase would not admit having any knowledge of the fire's origin.

Following this, Mr. Weaver reported the case to the State Fire Marshall's Office. Accordingly, Deputy State Fire Marshal Bruce Igou and Chas. E. Landis, Special Agent for the National Board of Fire Underwriters thereafter worked jointly with Chief Deputy Sheriff Bob Lawe in a further investigation. The following, in chronological order, is the information obtained.

During the early part of 1948, a series of fires occurred in the Lowell-Pinehurst district just south of Everett. Investigation of same by the Sheriff's Office, State Fire Marshal Smith and Chas. E. Landis, Special Agent for the MBFU, supplied information leading to the questioning of a recently discharged soldier, Harold Glen Chase, 19, who lived at 6005 Broadway, Lowell, Washington. Chase confessed to setting the fires for excitement; and at a later date signed a confession that he also had set a series of fires the year previously at Fort Meade,

Maryland. (Text regarding Chase's activity as sheriff's posse member is omitted here.)

Chase reported for work as night marshal about Tuesday, September 4, 1951. He secured for a room, the attic of a cabin at the Pine Tree Auto Cabins. The ground floor of the cabin was occupied by Ed Hunter, Jr., married son of the owner.

A night or two before the fire, Chase had occasion to question two local boys, James Niederprum and "Bud" Rymner, about some minor incident. According to these boys, they were questioned in the city hall. They further state that during the time they were there, Chase lit his cigarette lighter, placed it on the table and gazed at the flame; that later Chase lit a sheet of notepaper and watched it burn.

Mrs. Edna Walter, waitress in the Pioneer Tavern, claims that, the night before the fire, she heard Chase say to some customers, "Isn't there ever any excitement in this town". Chase later admitted this and added that he also had mentioned something about fire.

Larry S. Halling proprietor of the Pioneer Tavern, located diagonally across the street intersection from the scene of the fire, stated that at about 1:30 a.m. before the fire, (the fire alarm was at 4:03 a.m.), he saw Chase's police car parked at the east entrance to the alley where the fire later occurred.

At approximately 2:30 – 3:00 A.M., Chase, John Bates, brother of the fire chief, and Eddie Fortner, parked at the Union Service Station across the street from where the fire later occurred. Several bottles of beer were consumed. Bates claims to have gone home alone about 3 A.M. Chase offered to drive Fortner home. Enroute Chase, with Fortner as a passenger, chased a speeding car about 4 miles north of town. Returning to town, Chase let Fortner off in front of the high school. (Fortner lives in an apartment near the high school.) This time is estimated to be about 3:20 A.M.

Chase later claimed that he then started his final round of the night; that as he approached the post office he noted a car bearing a King County prefix license plate; that he questioned the occupants and was told that they were fishermen; that they had damaged their car and were looking for a repair garage so that they might have their car repaired after daylight; that he, Chase, directed them to a service station and garage across the road from the entrance to the aforementioned Pine Tree Auto Cabins.

Chase claims that he completed his rounds of the town, then drove north of town one mile as far as the saw mill; that he encircled a large machine shop building across from the mill; that he then drove south toward town and enroute turned into the entrance of the Pine Tree Cabins and thence about 500 feet to his cabin; that he climbed the outside stairs to his attic room and that, as he was pushing open the door, he happened to glance over his shoulder and then saw a glare of fire in the direction of town; that he then returned to his car and drove rapidly to town and directly to the City hall where he turned on the fire siren and then drove the fire truck outside; that he turned the fire truck over to Walter Bates, the fire chief, who had just arrived; that he then proceeded to the fire and thereafter directed traffic and guarded other stores from looting.

Chase, after several hours of questioning by Deputy Sheriff Bob Lawe, Deputy State Fire Marshal Igou and Chas. E. Landis, refused to admit that he had any knowledge of the fire's origin. By request, Chase drew a map purportedly showing the route he took on his rounds after leaving Fortner. Chase was released temporarily, pending further investigation.

Deith and Duane Morgan, local young men, admitted that Chase had stopped them for speeding on the night in question.

John Bates and Eddie Fortner verified those portions of Chase's story pertaining to themselves, except that whereas Fortner claims that he left Chase between 3 A.M. and 3:20 A.M., Chase claims that the time was between 3:40 A.M. and 3:45 A.M.

Dave Neyhart, Seattle, stated that he and Bill Meyer were in the car stopped by Chase about 3:30 A.M. the night of the fire; that Chase directed them to the garage and service station across from the entrance to the Pine Tree Cabins; that they, after leaving Chase on the main street; drove to the garage and parked in front of the garage; that Meyer had been drinking and went right to sleep; that he, Neyhart, had not yet gone to sleep when a car was driven past at a fast speed; that the driver was hollering "fire" and sounding his horn; that he is sure that it was the police car (Chase)that he saw; that the car turned toward town; that he got out of the car and looked around but could see no sign of fire.

Ed Hunter, Jr., previously mentioned as occupying the ground floor of the cabin where Chase lived, stated that every morning prior to the fire he always heard Chase, about 3:30 or 4 A.M., climb the stairs to the attic; that neither he nor his wife heard Chase the morning of the fire.

Ed Hunter, Sr., owner of the Pine Tree Cabins, who lives in the cabin nearest the entrance, stated that he had occasion to get up at 4 A.M.; that he smoked a cigarette before returning to bed; that about 5 minutes later, before he had gotten back to sleep, he heard the fire siren; that he looked out and saw that there was a fire in town.

Mr. Hunter is certain that Chase did not drive his car in or out of the driveway that morning.

Occupants of other cabins along the driveway were interviewed and stated that they heard no cars at or about the time Chase claimed to have been there.

One of these tenants was Mrs. John Fox, Cabin #16, which is located at a sharp bend in the driveway. In this connection, Chase had claimed that because of the high speed he was driving, enroute to the fire, that he had overdriven the curve and run over into a flower garden and that he had made considerable noise while backing out. Mrs. Fox and an adjacent occupant stated that they did not hear this. Incidentally, there is no flower garden at the point mentioned.

Mrs. Thomas F. Henson, wife of the owner of the Red Top Tavern destroyed in the fire, stated that she and her husband live about one block from the fire; that they were awakened by the fire siren and that they both went to the fire, she arriving a few minutes after her husband; that a few minutes after she arrived, Chase walked by and she asked him who had reported the fire and who had turned in the alarm; that Chase told her that he did not know and that he had gone to his room and was just starting to undress when he looked through the window and saw the fire.

Chase changed this story later to the effect that he had seen the fire when he glanced over his shoulder while opening the door to enter his room.

An examination of Chase's quarters revealed that there is no window on the side nearest town; that there is no glass in the door; that the lone window in the attic is on the west side and there is no direct view through same because of a large hot-water tank installation at that point.

It was further determined that it is almost one-half a mile in a direct line from the top of the outside stairs to Chase's room to the place where the fire occurred; that there is a heavy growth of second-growth fir trees in the direct line of vision from the stairs, some completely obscuring a view of the involved buildings.

In as much as the glare of a large fire could be seen over these trees, an effort was made to determine the length of time it would take Chase to descend the stairs, start his car and drive same to the City Hall and sound the alarm. His own estimate was three to four minutes, and investigators believe that to be the absolute minimum.

Along the same line, one 'Brick' West, former deputy sheriff who lives about 150 feet directly north up the alley from the fire, stated that he and his wife were awakened by the siren; that he slipped on a few clothes and then ran directly to the fire; than on his arrival he noted that the fire was entirely confined to the lean-to enclosure around the previously mentioned fuel oil tank; that the fire was fairly small and could not be seen from any great distance, except from a direct view; that the flames were just breaking through the shingle roof of the lean-to and were, at that time, well below the roof level of the adjoining buildings proper; that there were no flames inside of the buildings proper (this was verified by Chief Bates and others).

Mr. Doug. Laddusaw, who lives a few doors closer to the fire than Brick West, stated that he was awakened by the siren, and first went out to the front of his house, but could not see any signs of fire; that he then went out to the back of his house and then saw Mr. West passing enroute to the fire; that he had a direct view of the fire from his rear yard about 100 feet from the fire; that the flames then were quite small; that they were in and around the previously mentioned fuel oil tank; that they could not at that time have been observed more than a couple blocks and then only if one had a direct and unobstructed view.

It is estimated that at least two minutes elapsed from the time West and Laddusaw heard the siren and the time they arrived at the scene of the fire. This would be approximately 5 or 6 minutes after Chase claimed to have first seen the fire, and the investigators are of the opinion that it would have been impossible for him to have seen the fire from his cabin at that time.

Dr. P. R. Newkirk, previously mentioned as having handled Chase's case at the Northern State Hospital in 1948, was interviewed. He was asked the hypothetical question "Might Chase, knowing that he would be the prime suspect in the event of a fire, surrender to an 'urge' and deliberately set a fire." Dr. Newkirk stated that if the 'urge' occurred that Chase would not be restrained by the possible consequences of his act. In 1948 Dr. Newkirk had Chase listed as "Pyromaniac – Psychopathic."

Chase was picked up and again questioned by Deputy Chas. Law, Deputy State Fire Marshal Igou, and Chas. E. Landis. The various discrepancies in his story were pointed out. This had no apparent effect on him except that he tried to change his original statement to fit the circumstances. He now claimed that he first saw the fire as he drove down the driveway toward his cabin; that he saw the fire as he reached the aforementioned sharp turn; that at that point he had made the rapid turn that caused him to leave the road.

Chase was confronted with the fact that there was from 15 to 30 minutes, in his night's activities, that he had not accounted for. In reply, he said that he had spent approximately that amount of time at the home of a local Waitress. (This was later proved false).

The day following this interview, Chase notified the Sheriff's office that he had retained the services of a local attorney and that he would answer no further questions. However, he was induced to go to the Seattle Police Department. After arrival there, September 17, Chase agreed to take a 'lie-detector' test. The original test was given by Police Captain Clyde Dailey, following which he gave a recheck test. Then Captain Dailey assigned an assistant to give Chase another test, also followed by a recheck. Although Captain Dailey did not tell his assistant the result of his own test, both officers came up with the same answer, namely, that Chase had not told the investigators everything about the night of the fire, and that he was lying when he said that he did not set the fire. Incidentally a wire recording was made of the entire interview.

The evening of September 19, 1951, Chase was questioned, in the presence of his father, by Prosecutor Phil Sheridan, Deputy Prosecutor John Walsh, Deputy Sheriff Lawe, Deputy Fire Marshal Igou and Chas. E. Landis. At that time everything developed during the investigation was gone into. Case, as he did during the lie detector' test, would only admit "I might have set the fire, but I don't remember it". (sic)

It is of interest to note here that when Chase was being questioned about his "urges" he stated, "often, when I am driving down the highway, I have the urge to drive into someone walking beside the road, but I never do".

September 21, Mrs. Chase phoned Under-Sheriff Weaver and told him that his son was running away and that he was going to take the 10 A.M. bus out of Seattle for an unknown destination in California. Mr. Chase was crying as he made this report. Later neighbors reported to Deputy Sheriff Ed Walker that Mrs. Chase had told her son not to admit anything and that he would not have gotten into trouble in 1948 if he had just kept his mouth shut. Deputy Sheriff Law, after receipt of this report from Mr. Chase, proceeded at once to Seattle and contacted Detective Dick Wolph. Two married sisters of Glen Chase were contacted. Both stated that Chase had been there earlier that day and that he had told them that he was going to California after he disposed of his car. They appeared to be very much concerned.

After a consultation with the local parole board, a pick-up order was issued for Chase. Subsequently, the girl allegedly involved with Chase in the morals case was picked up and lodged in jail. Chase now faces a felony charge in that case.

An important factor in the case is the probability or lack of probability of the fire being of incendiary origin. In this connection, there has been no physical evidence found which would definitely establish the origin of the fire. On the other hand, M. Henson, proprietor of the Red Top Tavern who owned the fuel oil barrel around which the fire apparently originated, stated that the only storage, inside the enclosure around the tank, was some empty cartons; that there were no electric wires in or near same; that n one had been in the enclosure the evening of the fire. Incidentally, the fuel oil contained in the tank is not subject to spontaneous ignition.

For the record, it should be stated that there were rumors that lights had been observed in the rear part of the shoe repair shop late the night of the fire. However, no one has been questioned who would admit having actually seen any lights, and, as pointed out previously, early arrivals at the fire, state that there were no flames inside of the buildings at that time.

In this same connection, Mrs. Edna Walter, employee at the Pioneer Tavern, stated that she saw Mr. and Mrs. Purcell, proprietors of the shoe shop, in the Pioneer about 4:30 or 5 PM before the fire; that she heard Mrs. Purcell tell her husband that they had better get back to the shop, as the machine was running and the place might burn down; that Purcell replied "Let the damn place burn".

Maurice F. Purcell and his wife Diane were questioned separately and deny that they had made such remarks. They claim that they returned to the shop from the tavern, then went home; that Purcell went back to the shop about 5:30 P.M. to deliver a pair of shoes to a customer; that he then went home and was not again in the shop.

Under questioning, Purcell admitted that his shoe repair business has been poor and that he is now working for a logging firm. He stated that he had not left any machinery running and that he does not know of any accidental reason for the fire.

Orlie L. (Buck) Ennis, employee of the Bonneville Power Project, was checked as a possible suspect in connection with the fire. A fellow worker, Ian Duke, stated that he worked with Ennis on power line projects out of Arlington, Washington, and Darrington; that Ennis previously had worked on similar projects near El Centro, California and in Montana; that fires of unknown origin were said to have occurred at the latter places while Ennis was employed there; that Ennis was living at the Evergreen Hotel in Arlington at the time it burned about one month or so prior to the Darrington fire; that Ennis's conduct regarding fire is very queer; that Ennis, about 25, is originally from Texas.

A check with the contractor on the power project near Darrington reveals that Ennis, a wireman was fired September 5, 1951, three days before the Darrington fire. Also that Ennis checked out of a local hotel at that time and has not since been seen. His home address is shown on the company records as Box 666, Roseburg, Oregon. His Social Security number is (*number omitted by author*). Additional inquiry of Ennis will be made.

A further report will be made.

CHAPTER 32

Later in the same letter, Sullivan and Smith briefly summarize Chase's course.

In supplemental report of April 21, 1952, it was mentioned that Chase had admitted three murders and that he had been charged with two of them.

Chase subsequently was tried in Skagit County for the death of Leonard M. Lewis. According to later reports, this case was poorly prepared and he was found not guilty.

A few months later (about September) Chase, while in county jail in Everett awaiting trial for the murder of Dr. Bradley, again attempted jail break but was unsuccessful. On that occasion, an attempt was made to saw through his cell bars with a hacksaw blade which had been smuggled into the jail for him.

Later in the month, Chase's attorney, Paul Stocker, came to Prosecutor Phil Sheridan, according to the latter, and said that his client would plead guilty to the arson charge provided that the murder charge was dismissed.

Mr. Sheridan pointed out to Stocker that inasmuch as there is no statute of limitations on first degree murder that such an arrangement would not hold good if, at some later date, a new prosecutor decided to try Chase for the murder. As an alternative, Mr. Sheridan proposed reducing the charge to second-degree murder and, in addition, dismissing the arson charge. This met with Mr. Stocker's approval.

At a later date, Chase pleaded guilty to second-degree murder, and Judge Charles Denney sentenced him to life imprisonment with a recommendation to the parole board that Chase be confined for the rest of his natural lifetime. About October 2, 1952, Chase was taken to the state penitentiary at Walla Walla.

Recent reports are that he now is a full-fledged sex pervert.

Respectfully submitted,
Assistant State Fire Marshall
January 8, 1953

CHAPTER 33

From 1952 through 1959, Chase's first seven years in the penitentiary were relatively unremarkable. He had a good conduct and work record, and interestingly, he learned how to be an optician. He suffered a variety of minor injuries, but was never allowed to spend as much time in the hospital as he had when he was in the army.

He saw a different psychiatrist once a year from 1956 through 1958. The psychiatrist who evaluated Chase in October 1958 concluded, "I get the general over-all impression that the inmate is buckling down to business in an effort to make a better go of it in this life. I think hope should be held out for him and continued counseling and guidance offered. Diagnostically I would characterize him as an impulsive character disorder but not psychotic."

In his annual progress report dated October 15, 1959, the counselor concluded:

Evaluation: Chase's mental balance is in doubt and his weird actions of the past are unexplained. The inmate is definitely a good institutional charge and has established a superior work and conduct record.

Chase is talkative and presents a good picture verbally. There is an underlying feeling of innocence expressed by Chase and this is a question as to whether he actually accepts the fact that he is guilty of the crime for which he is committed. This person's unstable background is indicative of the individual's unstable personality and serious mental conflicts. His rationalizations for his activities are weak.

Chase's institutional record is good, work wise, but leaves much to be desired in helping the inmate solve his personality problems. The inmate mentioned that he has had the opportunity to see Dr. Sutch, institutional psychiatrist, on several occasions (there is no verification of this or reports of these contacts).

Chase's stability and parole ability is questionable.

Interestingly, there are no reports from Dr. Sutch dated prior to October 1959 in Chase's archived prison record either. However, Chase did see Dr. G. Charles Sutch four months later, on February 25, 1960. The note indicates that it was actually the first time he had met Chase. An excerpt from Sutch's note on that date suggests that he may not have paid close attention to the details of the case and did not want to spend the time listening to what Chase wanted to tell him.

He has been sentenced to the Washington State Penitentiary on a second-degree murder of a person by the name of Dr. Bradley, who was a dentist (author's note: Dr. Bradley was an optometrist) from Everett, and who allegedly was a homosexual. It is alleged by the inmate that he had a verbal argument with this particular man by the name of Dr.

173

Bradley, because he had made a homosexual advance toward the inmate and the inmate got angry and struck him in the judo fashion across the larynx. It was later revealed that after the body of Dr. Bradley was exhumed one year later, he had a fractured larynx.

At this particular point, it became quite apparent that the data and the evidence and information that the inmate was going to present to us was going to be long and complex and detailed, and because of the fact this inmate is relatively above average in intelligence and has an extremely fine verbal facility and besides, he works in the hospital division of the penitentiary, it was felt that it would be best if he would dictate on the Dictaphone a complete account of the event that ultimately led to his being put into the Walla Walla State Penitentiary. This particular dictation should be typed by a trusted stenographer and one copy, no carbon copies, should be made of the material that he produces, which will be presented to myself for evaluation and examination, and I will plan on seeing this inmate the next time I come to the penitentiary and complete my psychiatric examination, including the material that he has presented us with. I am very much impressed at this time by the sincerity of this particular inmate and perhaps, for the first time, we will get a factual account of everything that had taken place.

This note from the prison psychiatrist is the first direct inference in all available records that suggests Dr. Bradley may have been homosexual. Earlier, it was speculated that there might be a reason for some of his unexplained absences besides alcohol. If he were homosexual, the stigma associated with it in the 1950's would have ruined him. It is possible that he chose to be labeled an alcoholic to hide his sexual activity. It is also possible that the pressure to hide the fact contributed to his drinking.

CHAPTER 34

Dr. Sutch saw Chase a month later on March 24, 1960. Sutch discusses the dictation by Chase in this excerpt from the visit note completed on that date.

He has followed my suggestion and he has now dictated and the material he has dictated has been transcribed and it is currently in my possession. I would say that he has something like 150 to 200 typewritten pages, which represents a complete recital about such factors as history of early development, young adult life and the various problems and difficulties that he has become involved with in one way or another.

In this particular situation, I am informed by Dr. Heffron and some of the inmate nurses that while this inmate was dictating this material, he became profoundly involved emotionally with the recall and the listening back of some of the material that he had dictated. I regard this as good sign, which probably indicates that this inmate Chase has been a great deal sicker psychologically than we have previously surmised and that he most likely is treatable.

Dr. Sutch had asked Chase to dictate a note about the event that led to his incarceration. Chase dictated over 200 typewritten pages, included events from his entire life and was observed to become profoundly emotional upon recalling some of the events that he described. While this would seem to describe a person with obsessive traits, inability to follow directions, lack of focus and emotional instability, Dr. Sutch somehow concluded from this exercise that Chase was treatable.

CHAPTER 35

D r. Sutch returned to see Chase two months later on May 26, 1960, having read his dictated report. They discussed Chase's childhood. The following paragraphs are quoted from Sutch's report.

He states that his father was an auto mechanic and welder, and that they lived in a small house consisting of four rooms. The parents, both the father and the mother, two sisters, a brother and the patient all lived in this very small dwelling place. The patient had two sisters and one brother, besides himself. The brother was 1-1/2 years older than the patient; the sister Gail was four years older than the patient and the other sister, Francis, was eleven years older.

Due to the close proximity to each other, they were all in the same room and Gail, the youngest sister, the patient and the brother all slept in one bed. There was a considerable amount of sex play between them, most of which was instigated by the sister, and I might add that the patient during this time was the youngest of the four siblings. The patient also went on to state that prior to coming to the Penitentiary, he describes himself as being an almost complete nut and during this period was very suggestible, impulsive and apparently exercised very poor logic and judgment over many of the things that he may have done. For example, in 1949 he set fire to his own car and was caught almost immediately, red handed, but he got out of this situation by accepting a voluntary commitment to the Northern State Hospital for a period of three months, for the purpose of psychiatric observation. He claims at this time, due to his own choosing, that he completely fooled one of the staff psychiatrists there, told the staff psychiatrist only what the psychiatrist wanted to hear, and also made the psychiatrist believe that he had actually hypnotized him, when this had not taken place, and the psychiatrist actually wrote a lengthy report of some kind or another to indicate how he had cured this difficult patient of his troubles through hypnosis.

It would appear that Chase was actually fooling Dr. Sutch with his tale. It will be recalled that Chase went to Northern State Hospital for three months in 1949 because of a series of fires he confessed to setting in the Pinehurst neighborhood of Everett a year earlier, after he left military service. When Chase was discharged from Northern State, the psychiatrists did not consider him cured, but instead recommended that he receive a minimum of one year of psychotherapy. It also appears that information transfer to the prison record was poor, and that Sutch was depending on Chase's testimony for information.

The inmate at the present time is in the Penitentiary for the crime of second-degree murder, with a maximum sentence of fifty years, having murdered a dentist by the name of Dr. Bradley. (Author's note: Dr. Bradley was an optometrist.) The patient, even now, has some obsessive doubt as to whether or not he really did kill this individual, but admits to having struck the victim and that the victim did lie still and did collapse, seemingly, in the car at the time. (Author's note: Dr. Bradley was dead when brought to the hospital by Chase.)

This particular patient actually confessed to a series of five murders to the authorities...one was while he was allegedly at the Northern State Hospital and which he confessed erroneously that he had strangled a man, and it was later discovered that this was a lie and that actually the man had committed suicide. He was tried for this particular alleged crime and was acquitted by a jury.

(Author's note: It is true that Chase was acquitted by a jury in his murder trial of Leonard Lewis, but the subsequent finding of the same fracture of the laryngeal cricoid cartilage in Dr. Bradley suggests that the jury may have been wrong.)

In the army he did set two fires at various places, neither one of which was very significant, however, in the way of material damage or any loss to life. At this time the patient indicates that he knows only actually of five to six definite fires that he definitely did deliberately set.

(Author's note: This is in sharp contrast to the nine acts of arson that Chase was suspected of committing while he was in the army and later confessed to setting. One fire involved a death and one caused approximately $100,000 in damage.)

Today, during the psychiatric examination, it was my opinion that there has been a definite change for the better. The individual is showing some signs of developing maturity. The mere fact that he has actually taken the trouble to dictate a manuscript of approximately 300 pages, in which for the first time, he has told the valid facts as they really existed, instead of giving a snow job to whoever it was that was interviewing him, is indicative of the altered orientation and the motivation of this particular inmate. I really believe now, for the first time, he is making some sincere efforts at helping himself.

It is impossible to know what made Sutch think that on that day, for the first time in Chase's life, he had chosen to tell the truth.

CHAPTER 36

C hase and Sutch next met three months later on August 31, 1960, their fourth interaction. In his note from the meeting, it is clear that Dr. Sutch had come under Chase's powerful influence. He described Chase in favorable terms and suggested possible explanations for his behavior.

The patient was seen today in an extended interview, the first that he has had since my last dictation. It is my impression that this individual for the first time in his checkered kaleidoscopic career is making some real attempts at trying to understand his past behavior, especially those that were of an antisocial nature, that ultimately led up to his incarceration at the Washington State Penitentiary.

There was one interesting point that he mentioned in the interview today that will certainly have to be investigated a little more fully and that is the fact that at a very young age, when he was in one of the Armed Services, while on sentry duty this particular inmate was struck a very severe blow upon the occiput of his skull. He was rendered unconscious, the exact amount of time that he was unconscious is not known and to this very day there is an actual depression in the occipital region of his skull where he had been struck. The bones weren't actually fractured at that particular time but there is a depression from where he had received the blow. This particular head injury was inflicted upon him at a time long before he began the sequence of events that eventually led into antisocial conduct and behavior. Therefore, I shall attempt to talk to Warden Bob Rhay to see if something can be done in the way of arranging a neurological and electroencephalographic examination on this inmate. It would perhaps be most convenient to send him into Richland and have Dr. Dumke, our neurosurgeon, do this. This may have some bearing upon this individual's past behavior.

Author's note: Chase was struck in the back of the head with a crowbar while on guard duty at Aberdeen Proving Ground on September 25, 1946. His antisocial conduct and behavior actually appears to have begun only six months later when the first of several fires that he later confessed to setting at Fort Meade occurred. There is no evidence in his archived prison record that the encephalographic, neurosurgical, or radiographic evaluations were ever pursued.

It is also of interest that sometime after he had left the State Psychiatric Hospital where he was undergoing observation when picked up, apparently for something else, he voluntarily gave a confession that he had killed a patient at this State Hospital when in actuality he had not done anything like this at all. He was tried on this particular offense but his defense attorney was able to prove by all the people that were present and by calling upon various members of the staff that the man had died from other natural causes.

Author's note: In fact, the "something else" for which Chase was arrested in this case was first-degree arson in the town of Darrington, where he was employed as town marshal. When Chase was tried for the murder of Leonard Lewis, his attorney did not depend upon hospital staff for Chase's defense, but rather on an expert witness who was unable to draw any conclusions about Leonard's fractured larynx due to its advanced state of decomposition, despite the fact that the prosecution's expert testified that laryngeal fracture never occurs without a direct blow to the larynx. Finally, no one suggested that Leonard died of "natural causes." His death was attributed to suicide by strangulation with a pillowcase. Chase continued to mislead Sutch.

> The inmate at this time readily admits to have lied and having manipulated various types of situations that he was in in the past but is trying his best to tell the story the way it actually was instead of the way he had formerly carried out his actions. He even succeeded in actually misleading two psychiatrists.

Author's note: Actually, it would appear that three might be a more accurate number.

CHAPTER 37

The Progress Report from Chase's October 1960 annual review notes the availability of psychiatric reports by Dr. Sutch but describes them as being too verbose to include in the Progress Report. It does quote Dr. Finlayson, who, in 1957, said,

> Chase is an extraordinarily imbecilic character whose personality organization is at least, at times, very poorly oriented with respect to reality.

The report goes on to state that Chase was studying the Catholic religion and occasionally sang in the Catholic choir, despite the fact that he claimed to be Protestant when admitted to the penitentiary. The report said Chase continued to work in the prison optical department, he was a blood donor and inmate director of prison blood drives, and he claimed to have $5,000 in outside savings from his father's estate (unverified).

In conclusion, the counselor wrote:

> This individual is very talkative, verbalizes very easily, and on the whole presents a good picture verbally. He approaches life in an immature

and somewhat childish manner and reacts to many of life's problems in a very simple manner. His background history is unstable and reveals his immature and childish personality. His own rationalizations work for him adequately and there remains serious doubt in this person's mind as to whether he actually dealt the fatal blow that cost the victim his life.

Parole in this case will always be somewhat of a gamble as it is in most other cases and Chase's overall parole ability will not improve to any great extent. His chances of making a parole today will be about the about the same as it will 10 years from now.

It is interesting that the counselor was beginning to hint that parole was in Chase's foreseeable future, despite his past and ongoing behavior.

CHAPTER 38

Chase's mother died at the Mayo Clinic on November 4, 1960. It is unclear how her family could afford to take her to the Mayo Clinic, as the Chases were not well-off. Chase had always been close to his mother and had planned to return to live with her after his parole, apparently not considering how old she would be after he served fifty years. Dr. Sutch wrote the following clinical notes after his fifth visit with Chase on November 16:

> There has always been a very close relationship between the patient and his mother, and he wanted very, very much to go to her funeral. What the inmate did not know was that upon the mother's death, the family contacted the Penitentiary and apparently informed the warden that on the basis of his past behavior, as they last knew him, they did not want him attending the mother's funeral for fear that he might become emotionally disturbed and upset and create quite a scene. Therefore, the inmate was not allowed to attend the mother's funeral. Because of this, he became somewhat angry and hostile and unfortunately, many other people felt that he was not being treated fairly and justly in this matter and seemed to feed the fuels of his anger.

He however, discovered at a later date, especially when his sister came to visit him, that the reason he was not allowed to go was because the family requested that he not be allowed to go, on the basis of the behavior as they last knew him. They have known very little about his recent improvement here at the Penitentiary. Immediately upon finding this out, the inmate went about and apologized personally to all the people to whom he had been hostile and angry in a very contrite and humble manner. He now realizes that he should have been a little more patient and should not have done this, and is genuinely regretful for the incident that had taken place...

Sutch went on to discuss how Chase was demonstrating "considerable improvement" and an "excellent attitude," and said, "He is responding to his treatment now about as well as can be expected."

CHAPTER 39

Sutch next saw Chase about a month later on December 29. After that meeting, he wrote:

This individual was seen for another time here by myself. He apparently got into some kind of an altercation recently. This was not an isolated phenomenon. There were many others that were involved here at the hospital. I understand that the situation has been building up, insofar as the pressure and the tension has been concerned, and the inmate was not involved in any markedly or exaggeratedly gross infractions of discipline, but apparently his work has not been as good as it has been in the past. Some of this may be due to increased stress, pressure and anxiety, due to the disturbing personal relationships that were in existence here at the hospital now for some period of months.

It seems that Sutch was looking for forces outside of Chase to implicate for the problems that occurred. He supported his confidence in the inmate when he noted, "The inmate feels that he can bring this thing under control rather rapidly, and will do everything in his power to do so."

CHAPTER 40

D r. Sutch returned to see Chase almost a year later, on October 5, 1961. Excerpts from his report speak for themselves without editorial comment.

There has been a tremendous change of attitude in this particular inmate. It is of importance to indicate that he has become a convert to the Catholic religion, and has been working very dedicatedly and sincerely with Father McCabe; about a week from the time this was dictated, he was going to have his first confirmation and the Bishop of the Diocese was going to come down to administer confirmation. I believe that inmate Chase is very sincere about his current religious beliefs and it was a tremendous decision for him to make.

He reports to me that he is not going to go back to Everett, where he had all of his previous difficulties. He thinks that he might ask for permission to settle somewhere in Alaska.

This inmate has been in prison now for well over nine years, and has definitely avowed that he will see to it that he never lands back here or in any other penitentiary again. He further indicated to myself that this is the first time he genuinely felt like wanting to leave the Penitentiary and to do well on the outside, so he will never have to see the inside of a prison again. I am inclined to believe that this man is very sincere, and has made some very strenuous efforts at rehabilitating himself and the likelihood at this time is quite good that he should make a good adjustment on the outside. This is something that I hope the Board of Prison Terms and Paroles will take into consideration.

The counselor who prepared Chase's progress report for the October 1961 Parole Board Docket generally agreed with Sutch. He wrote:

This inmate continues to make a satisfactory adjustment in the institution and appears, as reported previously, rather immature and childish with a simple-mindedness that is surprising in one that is his age.

This inmate is putting all the effort he can into showing that he can get along satisfactorily in this type of environment in an effort to prove that he can get along in any type of environment.

Actually, this inmate has progressed to the point where it is not believed that there will be any appreciable change in him insofar as readiness for parole is concerned, and it is anticipated that he will be just as successful now as later on a parole status. It is recommended, however, that his parole be in a smaller area where there are fewer pressures and the understanding guidance of members of his family.

The State of Washington Board of Prison Terms and Paroles met October 26, 1961, and cut his sentence dramatically, setting his parole date for June 28, 1962, less than ten years after he entered the penitentiary with a life sentence at age twenty-two. The board said Chase could not be paroled to the Puget Sound area.

CHAPTER 41

Alaska declined Chase's application for parole there because the state already had an excess of unemployed parolees with no promise of employment opportunities on the horizon. Since the board had excluded Puget Sound, Chase said that he would like to go to Pasco in central Washington State. He had no relatives for support there and would need to seek his own employment, suggesting that he would look for jobs as a welder, mechanic, or in the crop harvest. His parole date was pushed back to September 1962 while his future location was determined.

It appears that the parole board preferred that Chase be placed in an area with family support. Its next move was to retract the Puget Sound prohibition and make only the towns of Darrington and Arlington out-of-bounds. His definite parole date was set as September 18, 1962. Both Chase's sister, Frances, and his aunt, Helen H. Baldwin, offered to take Chase into their homes. Baldwin lived alone in a four-bedroom home in Woodinville (twenty-five miles northwest of Seattle) and operated a realty company from her home. She was quite eager to have Chase share her home, offering him the entire second story as an apartment, and proposing to employ him to help with maintenance. The parole board selected Woodinville as Chase's new home.

Chase was released from the Washington State Penitentiary on September 18, 1962, with $297.91 in his possession. He was paroled to the supervision of District Parole Officer Robert Powell in Seattle and was to report to him the following day. He was to reside with his aunt, Mrs. Helen Baldwin of Woodinville. He had spent nine years, eleven months, and fifteen days in prison.

CHAPTER 42

Chase reported to the Seattle parole office on September 19, 1962, as instructed. Parole rules were discussed with him and he received counseling regarding employment. He immediately found a job at Puget Sound Salvage and Equipment Company. His primary occupation there was metal salvage—repairing large pieces of equipment that required welding and cutting. He earned $2.80 per hour. His supervisor described him as a very competent, efficient, and dependable employee. Chase was a member of Teamster's Local #117, Warehousemen and Chauffer's Union.

It was originally planned that Chase would live with his aunt, Mrs. Helen Baldwin, in Woodinville. However, he found it more geographically convenient to live with his sister, Mrs. Frances Frack, and her husband in their home in the Ballard neighborhood of Seattle, a very nice residential area. Chase had his own bedroom and paid $20 weekly for room and board. In April 1964, he moved into a small, two-bedroom apartment further north in the city, paying $45 per month in rent, $15 less than other tenants of the complex because of his willingness to do repair work and remodeling of the building.

In November 1964, Chase reported that his social life was an occasional date and occasional attendance at a Catholic church in downtown

Seattle. He claimed to be studying Latin in order to understand the Mass better. He reported that his long work hours precluded other social activity.

During Chase's supervised period of parole, he did become romantically involved with a woman with three children and hoped to marry her as soon as he was given a Conditional Discharge from Supervision. However, on March 28, 1964, Chase found her in a hotel with her ex-husband. In a fit of frustration, he returned home and took an (words blacked out on public document) that he had been taking on prescription. He realized how foolish he had been, went to a nearby church, and summoned police. He was taken to King County Harborview Hospital, where he was treated overnight and discharged the following day without ill effects. The attending physician felt that his actions were sufficiently explained by finding his fiancée in bed with another man, as well as the loss of the considerable amount of money that he had spent on furniture and an automobile for the woman. This was apparently the only problem that arose during Chase's adjustment period.

For two years, Chase attended each of his monthly probationary supervision visits in a timely fashion. He worked for the same company for the entire time without incident. He also showed stability of residence. When all factors were considered, he was granted a Conditional Discharge from Supervision on December 18, 1964.

Author's note: Harold Chase's probation supervision records were obtained through a standard request to the Public Disclosure Department, Washington State Department of Corrections. The agency sent thirty-eight pages and withheld nine pages because they contained "medical information, mental health information, and/or drug and/or alcohol information."

CHAPTER 43

Harold Glenn Chase's life ended twenty years later in California. He died in Saint Joseph's Hospital on July 10, 1984, at the age of fifty-five. No information can be located about his whereabouts or actions during the intervening twenty years. At the time of his death, Chase lived in a 1,000-square-foot, single-family home built in 1945, across the street from a city park. On his death certificate, the cause of death was ascribed to an accidental overdose of amitriptyline (an antidepressant medication) and ethanol (alcohol) that occurred on July 9, 1984. The "places of injury" were listed as his home and a tavern eight blocks away. Interestingly, the death certificate lists his marital status as divorced. Searches of marriage and divorce records of both Washington State and California failed to reveal either. He was buried in Lodi Cemetery in Lodi, California.

CHAPTER 44

P reviously unknown to me before doing the research for this book was the fact that a serial killer murdered my grandfather, Russell R. Bradley. In this case the motive was money—$538 to be exact.

The traditional definition of a serial killer is an individual who has killed three or people in a period of over one month. In addition, there must be a "cooling off" period between each murder. The motive for killing is usually based on psychological gratification. Some, including the FBI, define a serial killer as one who commits two or more murders as separate events. The FBI states that motives include sexual gratification, anger, thrill, financial gain, and attention seeking. Often the murders are attempted or completed in a similar fashion. The victims may have something in common such as gender, age, appearance, or occupation.

Serial killers differ from mass murderers, who kill multiple individuals all at one time without a cooling-off period between killings. They also differ from spree killers, who commit murders in more than one location but sequentially, one after the other.

Serial killers typically have low/average intelligence (the median IQ was ninety-three in one large study), contrary to the popular belief that they have high intelligence. Chase had an IQ of one hundred. Serial killers may have trouble staying employed, resulting in the fact that they often have menial jobs.

The MacDonald triad describes three predictors of psychopathy. These include (1) fascination with setting fires, (2) involvement in sadistic activity, which often takes the form of torturing animals in childhood, and (3) bedwetting beyond the age of twelve. Serial killers often demonstrate one, two, or all three of these characteristics. In addition, they often suffered some form of abuse by a family member during childhood and were frequently bullied as children.

The exact number of murders committed by Harold Chase is a matter of conjecture. If you include those that he claimed at one time or another to have committed and those that he is suspected of committing, the total from my research is six. All victims were adult males. Chase claimed that when he was in the army at Fort Meade in 1947, he killed two men in a race riot in Baltimore in which a total of six died. Despite extensive research, I have been unable to document that such a riot occurred in Baltimore that year. Contact with the Cold Case Unit of the Baltimore Police Department yielded no unsolved murders of that type in 1947. Either Chase was fabricating the murders or they occurred under circumstances other than those he described. He very likely caused the death of Sergeant George Joseph Bohotch, the soldier who died when the company supply building at Fort Meade, in which he was sleeping, burned. Chase was suspected of setting the fire, but evidence was insufficient to accuse him. Records do indicate that he was in the Station Hospital on the date of the tragic September 1947 fire, but the malady from which he suffered and its acuity are unknown.

Chase admitted the murder of Leonard Lewis in Northern State Hospital but denied the charge in court. A jury subsequently found him not guilty. Since serial killers often repeat the same method to kill, and Chase strangled his subsequent victim as well, it seems unlikely that the strangulation death of Lewis was self-inflicted. This conclusion appears to be supported by the presence of a fractured larynx, apparently quite unusual in self-inflicted strangulation. Further, one would wonder how a psychiatric patient in restraints, who is trying to starve himself to death and therefore probably weak, could manage the suicidal act described.

There seems to be little argument that Chase murdered Dr. R. R. Bradley by strangulation, as he confessed. When Bradley's body was exhumed and autopsied thirteen months after his death, an amended death certificate was issued, changing the cause of death from "coronary thrombosis" to "strangulation." Interestingly, when the family viewed his body privately shortly after death, Dr. Bradley's wife, Helen, asked why his neck was so swollen and bruised. My mother recalls that she was told that such findings are common after death.

Prosecutor Sheridan did not publically release the autopsy findings when they became available, not wanting to "tip my hand to the defense" prior to Chase's anticipated murder trial. Chase confessed to strangling Dr. Bradley, and the revised death certificate following the autopsy lists strangulation as the primary cause of death. In the trial of Chase for the murder of Leonard Lewis, a great deal of weight was placed on the fact that his larynx was fractured. One would wonder whether the same was true with Bradley.

In fact, Bradley's autopsy results are at least partially available in the public record. In a letter dated February 26, 1952, from Prosecutor Phillip Sheridan to the Mutual Life Insurance Company of New York, complying with a request for information, Sheridan summarized the findings of the autopsy performed on the exhumed body of R. R. Bradley by

Dr. Charles P. Larson on January 6, 1952. Specific areas of relevant interest include:

The heart was well preserved and all of the coronary arteries were carefully examined. There was no evidence of coronary arteriosclerosis or occlusions. The myocardium, endocardium, pericardium showed no disease. The valves of the heart were normal.

The trachea contains a little mucoid material. The lungs were collapsed and rested against the posterior chest wall. There were numerous subpleural petichial hemorrhages. Cut surface of the lungs shows edema.

The abdominal organs were apparently normal. Liver—no cirrhosis.

The neck organs were removed for careful examination. The only positive finding in the neck organs involved the cricoid cartilage. Two fractures were noted in this cartilage, one on either side of the midline, the first one laid 9 mm. to the right of the midline and the second 5 mm. to the left of the midline. There was some evidence of hemorrhage into the connective tissue and ligaments below the fracture on the left side. This area of hemorrhage measures approximately 2 by 5 mm. The cartilage was saved for x-ray studies.

Result of x-ray examination of the cricoid cartilage…There is in this object a definite fracture extending through the ossified cartilage.

Anatomical diagnosis:

1. Bilateral fracture of the cricoid cartilage.
2. Hemorrhage in area of fracture of left side of cricoid.
3. Bilateral subpleural petichial hemorrhages with edema of the lungs.
4. No evidence of cardiac pathology.
5. No pathology noted in examination of other organs"

Summary: Death is the result of asphyxiation of strangulation.

When reading the evidence, it seems probable that Chase did also murder the tourist "Joe" while on the lam in San Francisco. Chase's descriptions of the geography and locale seem quite specific for someone not previously familiar with the area. Fragments of broken glass were found in the car Chase was driving when he claimed to have broken a bottle over Joe's head. The car seats and Chase's overcoat were stained, probably with orange soda pop. It certainly is conceivable that a body thrown into an area of open Pacific Ocean infested with sharks would never be recovered, especially without an immediate search. US Immigration was quite different sixty years ago than it is today. It did not seem surprising that a tourist could enter the country but not be noted to have left it.

Two documents in Sheridan's file are dated after the notoriety of "Joe's" murder was lost amid the other media coverage.

January 24, 1952
Memo by Ralph McDonald
San Francisco Inspector of Police
Subject: Richard Podhorsky

Phone call received from John Walsh, this date, that information had now been obtained from Harold Chase that the name of the victim of the alleged murder committed in or about San Francisco was Dr. Richard Podhorsky, that subject was from Zagreb, Yugoslavia, that subject had stayed at the Hotel Crane, San Francisco.

Pursuing this information a check was made with the Hotel Crane and it was ascertained that the subject did stay there checking in on October 2, 1951 and checked out October 6, 1951 staying for a total of four days. His bill was paid, no forwarding address left. The clerk who accepted the reservation and the manager have no recollection of subject. In other words he was just an ordinary guest at the hotel and nothing unusual about his stay there. However, upon registering, he did sign the address 816 5th Avenue, New York.

Furthering the investigation a letter was sent special delivery this date to the Police Department of the City of New York, explaining to them the facts and requesting a check be made by them of the address given (see copy of letter in file).

Further check made with the Immigration Office that took in the San Francisco area, no information available. Advice of the immigration authorities say that it is an almost impossible task to ascertain if subject had entered the U.S., however, a further effort will be made by communicating with the office in Washington. The Yugoslavian Consul was checked with no results. The Yugoslavian Sokal Club was contacted but subject not known to them. The Board of Education and the California State Teachers Association contacted with the thought that possibly in view of the fact of his occupation as a schoolteacher he may have contacted said parties; no information available. Check of the Missing Persons Detail made under name given; no information available. Information given to the Press in the hope that some publicity might assist us to locate subject or his whereabouts.

Mr. John Walsh notified.

January 24, 1952

Letter from San Francisco Chief of Police to New York Police Department

Dear Sir:

The Homicide Detail of our Department is currently making an investigation in connection with an alleged murder which reportedly occurred during the latter part of October or the first part of November in 1951.

Regarding this investigation we are very anxious to learn the whereabouts of Richard Podhorsky who may be the victim in this homicide. The only address available is 816 5ᵗʰ Avenue, New York. This address was obtained from a hotel registration form in this city and we have no idea as to what period of time subject may have stayed there.

Our information is that subject came from Yugoslavia, his occupation was a schoolteacher and he may have the title of "Doctor." We were able to ascertain that he was in San Francisco during the early part of October 1951.

At the present time Harold G. Chase is in custody in the State of Washington. He has admitted committing this murder. He further stated that after the murder he disposed of the remains by throwing the body over a cliff just south of San Francisco.

We are inclined to feel that this crime actually did happen. In view of the fact that the body has not been recovered we are very desirous to gain any information available.

Thanking you in advance and requesting that you direct any communications care of the Homicide Detail, Attention: Inspector Ralph McDonald.

Very truly yours,

Michael Gaffey

(San Francisco) Chief of Police"

Sheridan had located a sheet of paper in Chase's personal effects that appeared to come from the red book in which he had claimed to write Joe's name. When confronted with the paper and the name, Chase was quoted as saying, "Yeah, that could be him." It seemed for an instant that the mystery of Joe had been solved. The victim was a middle-aged European male (from Yugoslavia, not France) who was a schoolteacher. The excitement of that investigative success, however, did not last long. A check by New York authorities discovered that Dr. Richard Podhorsky was a well-known Yugoslavian chemist, alive and well at that time, living in Yugoslavia and teaching at the University of Zagreb. It appears that the mystery of Joe will remain just that.

CHAPTER 45

Whether one believes Chase killed two or six or more, he meets the criteria for a serial killer, having murdered multiple people with a cooling-off period ranging from ten to twenty-two months between killings. A psychiatrist from Northern State Hospital tried to explore Chase's reasons for killing and his feelings about murder in an interview conducted immediately after his major confession.

January 5, 1952

Everett, Washington

Interview with Harold Chase by Northern State physician

Doctor: What sort of an effect did it have on your thinking and feeling?

Chase: The other two I felt sorry about (Lewis, Bradley) but I didn't even feel sorry for him ("Joe"). He was a queer and I just hate a queer, don't know why I do.

Doctor: Hate queers?

Chase: I don't know why but I do.

Doctor: You haven't had any experience with them in your personal action?

Chase: No.

Doctor: The first two you felt sorry for. Why so?

Chase: I don't know, for a time after I had done the (illegible), I felt relieved but afterwards, I was sorry. I don't know why.

Doctor: What sort of relief?

Chase: A tension relief, just to relax.

Doctor: What would build tension up?

Chase: I don't know, just as though I were building up on the inside and I had to let go. Maybe it was that way, maybe it was to set a fire. Something like that, I don't understand it.

Doctor: Do you notice when the tension starts to build up?

Chase: I start getting a little nervous, I guess.

Doctor: What does it cause you to feel or do, when it starts to build up?

Chase: I feel crowded, as if people were pushing me around. I feel as if I am being cornered.

Doctor: Do you feel irritable as if you had to strike out at them?

Chase: No, not exactly, I feel sorry for myself more than I do anybody else. That's the way I put it.

Doctor: How long does it take this tightness or pressure to build up?

Chase: No certain amount of time.

Doctor: Minutes, hours, days, weeks or months?

Chase: Weeks, a month, some of the crazy things I do, I do in a row and then I may not do anything again for months. I go for quite a length of time and then I start doing it again. I don't know why.

Doctor: Have you tried to do anything about that build-up of pressure?

Chase: I thought something could be done while I was up at the hospital.

Doctor: Have any ideas of why that sort of effect got started on you? When it got started, where it got started?

Chase: I have put an awful lot of thought to it, back clear into my child-hood, and I can't remember anything that has happened along my child-hood until after I was in the service. The only thing I can think of was when I got hit with a crowbar in the back of the head. If it was after that I don't know, if that was the case or not.

Doctor: What sort of wallop did you get on the head?

Chase: I was on guard duty there at Fort Meade, the Aberdeen Proving Ground down in Maryland and a guy comes up behind me and hit me with a crowbar.

Doctor: Hit you with a crowbar?

Chase: Hit the back of my helmet liner.

Doctor: What aftermath did you have from that? How did it affect you?

Chase: Headache and amnesia a little tiny bit. A bad blackout spot, nor exactly amnesia, but I didn't know exactly what was going on. Drowsiness a little bit, and I would get tired.

Doctor: Were there any medical findings as a result of it?

Chase: Well it was in my army record, my stay at the hospital, I rested up and then went back into the company.

Doctor: What made you decide to talk about the murders now?

Chase: Kinda funny. I always thought I was a tough guy, but I got so I was dreaming about them and they were bothering me quite a bit. It seems funny but they did. I would get nightmares about them.

Doctor: What did you dream?

Chase: Dream about all that was going on and see them laughing and see myself walking and put my hands around their necks and things like that. It used to scare me.

Doctor: Wake up?

Chase: Wake up in a cold sweat.

Doctor: Think something like that is going to happen to you or what? Why were you afraid of them?

Chase: I didn't think it was going to happen to me but it bothered me.

Doctor: Repeatedly wake you up in the middle of the night or just occasionally?

Chase: Getting pretty regular and worse.

Doctor: What were you afraid of as a result of that?

Chase: I was afraid I was losing my mind completely.

Doctor: Do you think you have ever been crazy?

Chase: There has to be something wrong with me. It must not be natural or I wouldn't do these things.

Doctor: When did you set your first fire, do you remember?

Chase: 1947

Doctor: 1947, yes, that was when you were in the service?

Chase: Yes.

Doctor: Was that after you got hit on the head?

Chase: Yes.

Doctor: Before that, had you any trouble at all in any sort of tangles with legal responsibility?

Chase: No.

Doctor: After this blow on the head, you began setting fires and playing the hero act?

Chase: Yes, I guess you could.

Doctor: Then the label "Firebug Chase"?

Chase: Yes, I guess so.

Chase's own motives for killing are less clear. If one were to believe all of Chase's testimony, financial gain was certainly involved in the cases of

Bradley and "Joe." One has to wonder whether there was a sexual aspect to at least some of his murders, as well. In the interrogation about his murder of Bradley on a deserted country road, Chase is able to recall very specific details more than a year later, such as the exact amount of money he stole from Bradley ($538) and the detailed directions to the Marysville cathouse to which they were supposedly headed. Yet when asked whether he had relations with Bradley, Chase replied that he could not remember. It also seems unusual that a fifty-two-year-old man entering a bar would choose to sit with a solitary twenty-one-year-old, and then proceed to surreptitiously show him a roll of money and suggest that they go elsewhere. Later, in one psychiatry note from Chase's Walla Walla record, the physician refers to Bradley as an "alleged homosexual."

When Chase went on the lam to San Francisco, he met the tourist "Joe" in a bar. Joe offered Chase money for his time as a city guide. The two ended up on the coastline near the Cliff Restaurant. They were also near the bathhouses located below the restaurant, which were popular with the gay community at the time. Before murdering Joe, Chase describes spending an hour with him in the car, watching the sun set. It certainly seems possible that Chase could have murdered some of his sexual partners in an attempt to deal with his personal psychological issues.

Chase fit the serial killer profile with regard to meeting at least one of the criterion of the MacDonald triad, that of fascination with setting fires. A review of available records indicates that he probably set at least eight fires while in the army at Fort Meade, another five in his neighborhood once he returned home, and then the major fire in Darrington. Arsonists are known for seeking attention and publicity. Often, they are the ones who report the fires they set, and it is not uncommon for them to help fight the fire. Chase did all of these things. It is particularly telling that he personally phoned the fire marshal after the last fire that he set in his neighborhood. It is hard to imagine more blatant attention-seeking behavior.

It is interesting that Chase was captured after only six weeks in San Francisco, yet he had eluded not only arrest, but even suspicion for some of his crimes for months to years. He must have known at a minimum that a warrant had likely been issued for his arrest on charges of parole violation when he left the state. Why, then, did he apply for a job at a federal government facility where providing his Social Security number would most certainly lead to a background check and discovery of his fugitive status, as it did? Did Chase want to be caught so that he could tell his fabulous story and gain notoriety? Many actions in his life seem to point to his desire for attention. Alternatively, did he feel invincible and that he would never be caught, no matter what he did? His criminal experience could have instilled that belief within him, since even when he was convicted of arson his sentence was suspended. Finally, maybe he just believed that the system was so broken that it would not catch up to him again. After all, as a convicted arsonist, he was able to join the county sheriff's posse and be deputized, hired as the marshal of a town, and successfully apply for a federal gun permit. Indeed, many systems were broken.

CHAPTER 46

Chase's history of head trauma should not be overlooked, as some studies have associated significant head trauma with violent behavior later in life. Violent behavior has been claimed to be associated with educational level, a rapidly changing society, genetic influences, and an interaction between genetic and environmental factors. Brain structure has not been well associated with violence, but brain function abnormalities are much more commonly seen in criminals. Such brain dysfunction may be the result of head trauma. In Chase's many narratives, at least two possible instances of traumatic head injury are described. As a youngster, he described falling down the stairs. His collarbone was broken; head trauma was not mentioned, although it could have occurred. In early military training, he was struck on the back of the head with a crowbar and hospitalized for weeks.

In a study by Leon-Carrion in Spain, differences between violent and nonviolent prisoners were examined. The factor that differentiated them was a history of untreated head injuries in childhood among those with histories of violent behavior. He also found that when head injuries are sufficiently severe to require hospitalization, the risk for serious, violent behavior increases.

Dr. Sarah Stoddard, of the University of Michigan School of Nursing, followed a group of 850 midwestern public school students for eight years in an attempt to identify characteristics associated with interpersonal violence in young adulthood. Participants who had experienced head injuries before young adulthood were more likely to be involved in interpersonal violence than those who had not.

Chase appears to have initiated interpersonal violence in young adulthood, claiming that he was never in trouble until he joined the army. If another soldier at Aberdeen Proving Ground hit him in the head with a crowbar as claimed, deduction places the injury on September 25, 1946, when Chase was seventeen, as discussed earlier. Until that time, his criminal record was clean. The first of a string of arson fires at Fort Meade took place on March 29, 1947, almost six months to the day following his head injury. From that date forward, violent activity was a part of his life.

A study in Sweden sought to examine links between traumatic brain injury and subsequent violent behavior using health databases of the country's population. "Violent behavior" was defined as conviction for homicide, assault, robbery, arson, any sexual offense, or illegal threats or intimidation. Researchers found that 9 percent of those experiencing traumatic head injury were subsequently convicted of violent crime. This was 3.3 times the rate of violence among those without head trauma. Unfortunately, the study did not break down the rate of individual violent crimes listed. Certainly, Chase's most common were arson and murder.

CHAPTER 47

C hase was not just a murderer and arsonist. In the course of research-
ing him, I have also noted and recorded claims or accusations of
assault and battery ("rolling queers" in San Francisco; the attack on the
Snohomish county jailer during Chase's escape attempt), robbery (of Dr.
R. R. Bradley, Joe in San Francisco, and "queers" in San Francisco), burglary (The Casino Tavern in Everett while a deputy in the Snohomish
County Sheriff's Posse), mail fraud (stealing his mother's government
checks), interstate flight to avoid prosecution (his escape to San Francisco
after the Darrington arson), and pornography production in Seattle in
1950.

When combined with the possibilities of up to six murders and four-
teen arsons, it seems an amazing amount of crime for one person to commit from 1947 to 1952, at ages seventeen to twenty-one.

Perhaps the thing most disappointing and difficult to understand
is how one individual was able to commit this string of crimes without being stopped. There are so many places in Chase's story where it
appears that someone should have sounded the alarm and stopped the
line.

Chase joined the US Army at age seventeen, dropping out of school after the ninth grade. When he appeared at Fort Meade and obvious acts of arson began at the same time, he was actually suspected of setting fires and calling them in. An effort was eventually made to monitor his nocturnal activities, but without success. How carefully were each of the first seven fires investigated? Why was he known as Firebug Chase? Sergeant George Bohotch died in the eighth fire. Could his life have been spared if the arsonist had been identified earlier?

Equally disturbing about his army career was the obvious psychological dysfunction that was tolerated, at least for one year and eight months. Chase spent fully one-half of his time hospitalized for seemingly minor injuries or on furlough. Unfortunately, his medical records are not accessible, so it is not possible to gain insight into what his physicians were thinking. As noted previously, it appears that Chase was hospitalized for long periods to keep him out of trouble, especially during the last two to three months of his time in the service, which he spent at Percy Jones Hospital in Michigan. Accessible records do note that his US Army discharge physical examination was entirely normal, including psychological and neurological examinations. He was transferred from Fort Meade because he was suspected of serial arson and, in fact, later in life confessed to setting fires there. Because it was not possible to collect the evidence, he was transferred to another location, placed in a holding pattern for a couple of months, and discharged.

Chase separated from the army with an Honorable Discharge. His last assignment was to the Detachment of Patients, Percy Jones Hospital, Battle Creek, Michigan. His records indicate that his separation was "For the convenience of the government (AR 615-365)." In the 1940s, this phrase and code was most commonly used as an administrative discharge for neuropsychological reasons.

Norman Brill summarized the way this evolved during World War II. During the early mobilization period of the war, the US Army was expanding rapidly. From the beginning, large numbers of men were admitted to the various station hospitals because of psychiatric disorders. Many were frankly psychotic or psychoneurotic; others were immature, mentally defective, or had personality or character disorders that interfered with their adjustment.

Generally, if a soldier consistently did not adjust at duty, he was referred to the hospital. Dispensary medical officers did little in the way of therapy. They were kept busy screening the many men who reported daily on sick call, trying to get as many as possible back to their duties promptly.

From the beginning of mobilization, psychiatrists were impressed with the poor motivation of many patients who found their way into hospitals. It was difficult to define exactly how much of such patients' ineffectiveness was due to illness and how much to lack of desire to do their part. Seemingly conscious exaggeration of existing defects was not uncommon.

Use of AR 615-365 for administrative vs. medical discharges varied from liberal to conservative during the war, and it was apparently the source of some confusion and dispute. War Department Circular 391, dated December 29, 1945, was published to clarify the capabilities of individuals being considered for discharge. While this came after the end of WW II, it was in effect when Chase was discharged in 1948. Following the statement that his separation was "for the convenience of the government," his papers read, "Physical incapacitation Par 2 c (2) WD Circ 391 dated 29 December 1945."

Paragraph 2 c (2) reads: "Those unlikely to render effective service upon return to duty by reason of likelihood of early recurrence of incapacitating symptoms as a result of continued military service, but who can be returned to civilian life without likelihood of such recurrence, will be transferred to the detachment of patients if not already so assigned, and ordered, on a duty status, to the separation center nearest their homes for discharge under the provisions of AR 615-365, and this circular."

It is very difficult to know how to interpret this in Chase's case. Was the army implying that his prolonged hospitalizations for seemingly minor problems was malingering to avoid duty and that this would pass once Chase returned to civilian life? Or was it talking about Chase's psychopathic activity as a suspected serial arsonist? If the latter, someone appears to have predicted quite incorrectly that such pathology would spontaneously remit after military discharge. Chase's behavior in the service was the first missed opportunity to identify his psychological problems and intervene.

After leaving the military, Chase returned to his Everett, Washington, home and proceeded to set fires throughout his neighborhood, eventually calling attention to himself as the arsonist, apparently for recognition. He was evaluated by a psychiatrist in Seattle, who concluded that, *"Under no circumstances should this individual be free on his own responsibility until therapy has brought about recovery."* He was then sent to Northern State Psychiatric Hospital for a three-month evaluation and recommendation. The hospital returned a confusing diagnosis and a vague recommendation for management. The court convicted him of the Everett arson fires and sentenced him to ten years in the State Reformatory. Had that sentence been carried out, none of the events in the remainder of this story, including my grandfather's death by strangulation, would have occurred. Instead, for reasons that are unclear, the court ignored the psychiatrist's opinion, suspended the sentence contingent upon his participation in ongoing outpatient psychiatric care, and set him free. The second opportunity to intervene was lost.

Why did people believe Chase's story when he brought Dr. Bradley's body to the hospital? There is no doubt that an autopsy would be required today for the unexplained, out-of-hospital death of such a young person. Why did everyone concur that Bradley died of a heart attack when he was young for heart disease, had hauled two deer out of the forest recently without difficulty, and his only suspicion for heart disease was a mildly elevated heart rate on prior examination?

Numerous individuals noted the abnormal post-mortem appearances of Leonard Lewis and Russell Bradley, yet this never led to suspicion of murder by the authorities. In the case of Leonard Lewis, family members described facial bruising, and a swollen throat. His brother-in-law even expressed the belief that his relative had been killed. The two sheriff's deputies who picked up Dr. Bradley's body described extensive blue discoloring of his face for such a short time since death. Bradley's wife noted that his throat was swollen to twice its normal size and discolored. She recalls that staff at the funeral home remarked on his unusual appearance. No investigation was pursued. Why was nothing done? It appears that a tremendous amount of circumstantial evidence pointing at Chase as a murderer was ignored, and thus, the third opportunity to intervene in his behavior was missed.

Despite the fact that extensive background checks were ostensibly performed when the Snohomish County Sheriff's Posse was formed in 1949, and applicants were required to be a minimum of twenty-one years of age, Chase appears to have been admitted sometime in early to mid-1949, at the age of twenty, with a felony conviction on his record. Sheriff Warnock apparently thought that being a member of the posse would help rehabilitate Chase. Along with the position came deputation, as members were required to perform a minimum number of Snohomish County deputy shifts monthly. It is impossible to understand the judgment used in this situation. What sense did it make to appoint a troubled youth to deputy status?

It was on his deputy duties that he learned the money-handling process for the Casino Tavern, allowing him to burglarize the establishment in the summer of 1959. It was in his posse uniform that he murdered my grandfather, according to prosecutor Sheridan's notes. If he were a member of the posse for the one and one-half years that he claimed, that would also encompass the time that he acted in the pornographic movie in Seattle. Missed intervention opportunity number four occurred when he was allowed join the sheriff's posse and partake in the opportunities for criminal activity that it gave him.

In early 1951, just weeks after murdering Bradley, Chase applied for and was granted a federal weapons license. He obviously then acquired a large handgun, as it is mentioned in several interviews. It is not known whether he subsequently used it in the commission of any crimes, but the fact that a license was issued is incomprehensible. Background checks appear to have been no better in 1951 than they are today. Perhaps being a member of the Snohomish County sheriff's posse and a deputy was sufficient to trump his felony arson conviction (to which he pleaded guilty) and the various psychiatric diagnoses he had accumulated.

As a felon on parole for arson, he was hired as marshal for Darrington, and then burned down a large portion of the business district. It would appear from newspaper accounts that his history as a posse deputy for Snohomish County helped him to get the job. Hiring an individual to protect your town, having him burn down a major portion of the business district, and then learning that you had hired an arsonist on parole is unfathomable. It seems that poor communication between governmental offices comprise the fifth missed intervention point.

Chase went to prison for the murder of my grandfather. With everything in his background, why wasn't Chase sentenced to life in prison *without possibility of parole?* And why was he released less than a decade later? The sentencing judge emphasized the risk Chase posed by writing about his extreme danger to society at the end of his sentencing document. The prison records indicate that psychiatrist Dr. Sutch believed that Chase was telling the truth when he minimized his crimes, raised doubt that he actually had committed the crime for which he was sentenced, and said that he would never pursue such activity again. The prison counselor who wrote Chase's periodic status reports implied that he might be ready for parole because he had reached maximum rehabilitation potential. Does that equate to being a good citizen in society? Does any of this make sense? While rehabilitation for an eventual successful return to society is a goal of imprisonment, isn't the punishment that comes with incarceration another goal?

These are the questions that run through my mind each spring when I take my outboard motor to the boatyard for tune-up. To get to the facility that I use, I drive north out of Everett on Old Highway 99, across the Snohomish River Bridge, and then take the first right turn after the bridge. I stop at the spot where my grandfather was strangled, get out of the car, and can see on the hill behind me View Crest Abbey Mausoleum, the place where my grandfather's body is entombed, forever overlooking that spot on Smith Island where he was murdered.

RESOURCES AND SOURCES

Personal interviews with Mary Louise Bradley (2010-2013) and Russell R. Bradley Jr. (2012), children of Russell R. Bradley.

Personal interviews in 2012 and 2013 with Joyce Jones resident, former mayor, and movie theater employee in 1951, Darrington, WA.

Telephone interview (2012) with Bob Ensley, resident and 1951 movie theater employee, Darrington, WA.

Personal interview (2012) with Donna Shroyer, resident at Utsalady Bay, Camano Island, WA, since 1934.

Telephone interview 2011 with police officer representative of Cold Case Unit, Baltimore Police Department, Baltimore, MD.

Telephone interview with Mike Radovich (2012), Lake Stevens, WA, Current member, Snohomish County Sheriff's Posse.

Telephone interviews with Chris Gee (2012 and 2013), Snohomish Historical Society and Snohomish County Sheriff's Posse, Snohomish, WA.

Personal interview in 2013 with Paul Stocker, defense attorney for Harold G. Chase's two murder trials, Everett, WA.

United States Census 1910, 1920, 1930, 1940. Accessed 2010-2013. www. Ancestry.com.

William Whitfield, *History of Snohomish County Washington*, Volume 1. (Chicago, IL: Pioneer Historical Publishing Society, 1928), 547.

Personal journal and correspondence written by R. R. Bradley.

Northern State Hospital Admission Register, 1949.
Accessed via:
James Copher, archivist
Washington State Archives: NW Region
Western Washington University, Bellingham, WA

Coroner's Record, Everett, WA.
Russell R. Bradley, Case No. 50-208-809
December 12, 1950
Archives of Snohomish County Prosecutor's Office, Everett, WA.

Case notes for R. R. Bradley murder prosecution (1952)
Phillip Sheridan, Snohomish County prosecutor
Archives of Snohomish County Prosecutor's Office, Everett, WA

Correspondence between New York City Police Department and Snohomish County Sheriff's Office, January 24, 1952.
Archives of Snohomish County Prosecutor's Office, Everett, WA.

Death certificate, Russell R. Bradley, December 12, 1950, Washington State Department of Health.

Revised death certificate, Russell R. Bradley, undated, Washington State Department of Health.

Military service records, Harold G. Chase 1946-1948.
Accessed via: National Personnel Records Center
1 Archives Drive
Saint Louis, MO 63138.

Statement of Harold Glenn Chase taken in the presence of Fire Marshal E. L. Smith and Chas. E. Landis, March 28, 1948. Accessed via Snohomish County Superior Court Records, case 915, 1948.

Statement written by Harold Glenn Chase discussing his role in neighborhood fires since his return from the US Army in February, 1948. Accessed via Snohomish County Superior Court Records for case 915, 1948.

Statement of Harold Glenn Chase taken in the presence of Tom Warrock, Phil Sheridan, John Walsh, Mr. McQuillin, and Norma Willet, stenographer. January 5, 1952, 1:00 a.m. to 3:00 a.m., twenty-eight pages in length. Accessed via:
James Copher, archivist

Washington State Archives: NW Region
Western Washington University, Bellingham, WA

Statement of Harold Glenn Case taken by unnamed physician from Northern State Hospital on January 5, 1952.
Archives of Snohomish County Prosecutor's Office, Everett, WA

Statement of Mrs. Helen Bradley Hart, taken before Sheriff James Warnock on January 7, 1952.
Archives of Snohomish County Prosecutor's Office, Everett, WA.

Statement of J.D. Lorraine, Snohomish County deputy sheriff, taken by Prosecuting Attorney Phillip Sheridan on January 17, 1952.
Archives of Snohomish County Prosecutor's Office, Everett, WA.

Unidentified reporter, "Car plunges into river at Darrington," *Everett Herald,* June 27, 1949, 1.

Unidentified reporter, "Bodies of Darrington youths found Monday," *Everett Herald*, June 28, 1949, 1.

Death notice. "Dr. Bradley dies suddenly here early Tuesday morning," *Everett Herald*, December 12, 1950, 1.

"Dr. Russell R. Bradley" obituary, *Everett Herald*, December 12, 1950, 6.

E. O. Walker, "Escape foiled," *Everett Herald*, January 5, 1952, 1.

Unidentified reporter, "Authorities checking on story of jail inmate regarding murder of Everett optometrist, two others," *Everett Herald*, January 7, 1952, 1.

Unidentified reporter, "Autopsy shows Bradley's death not natural. *Everett Herald,* January 8, 1952, 1.

Unidentified reporter, "Murder count to be filed against Chase," *Everett Herald*, January 8, 1952, 1.

Herald staff photographer, photograph caption, "Warrant served," *Everett Herald*, January 9, 1952, 1.

Herald staff photographer. Photograph caption, "Books attacker," *Everett Herald*, January 9, 1952, 19.

Unidentified reporter, "Arson trial for Chase is stricken from January jury calendar Wednesday," *Everett Herald*, January 10, 1952, 1.

Herald staff photographer, photograph caption, "Murder scene," *Everett Herald*, January 11, 1952, 1.

Unidentified reporter, "Jury chosen in Chase trial," *Everett Herald*, May 20, 1952, 1.

Unidentified reporter, "Chase trial opens today," *Everett Herald*, May 20, 1952, 1.

Lucille Cohen, "Sheriff relates Chase confession at murder trial." *Seattle Post-Intellingencer May* 21, 1952, 1.

Unidentified reporter, "Defense says Lewis sought to kill self," *Everett Herald*, May 23, 1952, 1.

Unidentified reporter, "Psychiatrist heard in murder trial," *Everett Herald*, May 23, 1946, 1.

Unidentified reporter, "Chase slated to speak in own defense," *Everett Herald*, May 24, 1952, 1.

Unidentified reporter, "Jury ponders fate of Chase in death trial," *Everett Herald*, May 25, 1952, 6.

Unidentified reporter, "Chase acquitted in murder trial by Skagit jury," *Everett Herald*, May 25, 1952, 1.

Unidentified reporter. "Chase facing life in penitentiary for killing of Dr. Bradley," *Everett Herald*, September 30, 1952, 1.

Lloyd Stackhouse, "Ex-town marshal at Darrington says he killed 3 men," *Seattle Post-Intelligencer*, January 6, 1952, 1.

Lloyd Stackhouse, "Murder charges filed in Everett doctor's slaying," *Seattle Post-Intelligencer*, January 9, 1952, 1.

Charles Regal, "Chase's father takes bible, food to jail," *Seattle Post-Intelligencer*, January 9, 1952, 8.

Unidentified photographer, photograph caption, "Arson," *Seattle Post-Intelligencer*, January 9, 1952, 8.

Lloyd Stackhouse, "Portrait of a confessed killer," *Seattle Post-Intelligencer*, January 10, 1952, 1.

Ken Harris, photograph caption, "Confessed slayer," *Seattle Post-Intelligencer*, January 10, 1952, 1.

Unidentified reporter, "State hospital at Sedro Woolley changes procedure for admittance of patients," *Seattle Post-Intelligencer*, January 10, 1952, 16.

Stan Glowacki, Confessor faces death charge," *Seattle Times*, January 8, 1952, 1.

Unidentified reporter, "Chase recommended by Sheriff's office," *Seattle Times*, January 9, 1952, 1.

Unidentified reporter. "Chase's 'crimes' imaginary, says mother." *Seattle Times*, January 10, 1952, 3.

Staff correspondent, "Body of second Chase 'victim' to be exhumed," *Seattle Times*, January 11, 1952, 4.

Unidentified reporter, "Man reported slain very much alive," *Spokane Daily Chronicle*,
January 25, 1952, 2.
Archived issues of *Seattle Post-Intelligencer* and *Seattle Times*
Accessed via:
Bo Kinney
Special Collections
The Seattle Public Library
Seattle, WA

Funeral notice for Harold G. Chase, *Stockton Register*, July 18, 1984.
Accessed via Delailah Little, Newsroom librarian, *Stockton Register*.

Snohomish County Superior Court record dated November 8, 1951, accusing Harold G. Chase of arson in the first degree in Darrington, WA, on September 8, 1951.
Accessed via:
James Copher, archivist
Washington State Archives: NW Region
Western Washington University, Bellingham, WA.

Snohomish County Superior Court record dated September 30, 1952, convicting Harold G. Chase of murder in the second degree and sentencing him to the state penitentiary in Walla Walla for life on hard labor.
Accessed via:
James Copher, archivist
Washington State Archives: NW Region
Western Washington University, Bellingham, WA.

Letter dated February 26, 1952, from Prosecutor Phillip Sheridan to the Mutual Life Insurance Company of New York.
Archives of Snohomish County Prosecutor's Office, Everett, WA.

T. W. McCallister, "Neuropsychiatric sequelae of head injuries," *Psychiatr Clin N Am,* 15(2), (1992): 395-413.

J. Leon-Carrion and F. J. Ramos, "Blows to the head during development can predispose to violent criminal behaviour: rehabilitation of consequences of head injury is a measure for crime prevention." *Brain Inj,* 17(3), (2003): 207-216.

S. A. Stoddard and M.A. Zimmerman, "Association of interpersonal violence with self-reported history of head injury," *Pediatrics,* 127(6), (2011): 1074-1079.

S. Fazel, P. Lichtenstein, M. Grann, and N. Langstrom, "Risk of violent crime in individuals with epilepsy and traumatic brain injury." *PLoS Med,* 8(12), (2011): e1001150.

Revised Code of Washington State w9.95.115. Parole of life term prisoners.

N. Q. Brill, "Military psychiatry in practice: Hospitalization and disposition," Office of Medical History, U.S. Army Medical Department, accessed February 20, 2013, http://history.amedd.army.mil/booksdocs/wwii/NeuropsychiatryinWWIIVolI/chapter9.htm.

War Department Circular 91, published December 29, 1945.

US Social Security Death Index (accessed via Ancestry.com)

Death certificate, Harold Glenn Chase, July 10, 1984. State of California Department of Vital Records.

Town of Darrington, Official website of the town of Darrington, WA, accessed February 20, 2013, http://town.darrington.wa.us/.

Glacier Park Lodge, Glacier National Park, accessed February 26, 2013, http://www.glacierparkinc.com/glacier_park_lodge.php.

The U.S. Army, the official homepage of Aberdeen Proving Ground, Maryland, accessed March 11, 2012, http://www.apg.army.mil.

Adriane Foss, Public Affairs Specialist
Garrison APG Public Affairs Office
Building 305, West Wing (IMAP-PA), Aberdeen Proving Ground, MD 21005-5001

U.S. Army Crime Records Center
27130 Telegraph Road, Quantico, VA 22134
Phone: 571-305-4224

Freedom of Information Act
U.S. Army Criminal Investigation Command, accessed March 27, 2013, http://www.cid.army.mil.

Walla Walla Penitentiary Commitment and Clemency Records

Accessed via:
Maggie Chamberlin, research assistant
Washington State Archives
1129 Washington Street SE, Olympia, WA 98504-0238

Prison Records 10/3/1952-9/17/62
Washington State Penitentiary at Walla Walla
Accessed Via:
Lupita Lopez and Molly Rooney, archivists
Washington State Archives
1129 Washington Street SE, Olympia, WA 98504-0238

Field File and Indeterminate Visit Review Board File
Washington State Department of Corrections
Accessed via:
Jamie Gerken, Public Disclosure Manager
Washington State Department of Corrections
Phone: 360-725-8282

Made in the USA
Charleston, SC
01 April 2014